Emotional Intelligence

The supreme guide on how to Improve your social skills, control your emotions and become more resilient , evolve your personality and build healthy relationships.

Copyright @2019 By Jeremiah Bonn

All Rights Reserved.

The following Book is reproduced below with the goal of providing information that is as accurate and as reliable as possible. Regardless, purchasing this Book can be seen as consent to the fact that both the publisher and the author of this book are in no way experts on the topics discussed within, and that any recommendations or suggestions made herein are for entertainment purposes only.

Professionals should be consulted as needed before undertaking any of the action endorsed herein.

This declaration is deemed fair and valid by both the American Bar Association and the Committee of Publishers Association and is legally binding throughout the United States.

Furthermore, the transmission, duplication or reproduction of any of the following work, including precise information, will be considered an illegal act, irrespective whether it is done electronically or in print. The legality extends to creating a secondary or tertiary copy of the work or a recorded copy and is only allowed with express written consent of the Publisher. All additional rights are reserved.

The information in the following pages is broadly considered to be a truthful and accurate account of facts, and as such any inattention, use or misuse of the information in question by the reader will render any resulting actions solely under their purview. There are no scenarios in which the publisher or the original author of this work can be in any fashion deemed liable for any hardship or damages that may befall them after undertaking information described herein.

Additionally, the information found on the following pages is intended for informational purposes only and should thus be considered, universal. As befitting its nature, the information presented is without assurance regarding its continued validity or interim quality. Trademarks that mentioned are done without written consent and can in no way be considered an endorsement from the trademark holder.

Contents

Introduction 7

Chapter 1 20

Emotional Intelligence Defined 20

    What Is Emotional Intelligence? 25

    The History of the Study of Emotional Intelligence and Different Models 30

    Controversy Surrounding Emotional Intelligence 36

    The Role of Emotional Intelligence 37

    Emotional Intelligence and Resilience 42

    Not Allowing Another's Mental State to Impact Your Own 45

    Societal Problems with Emotional Intelligence 48

    Emotional Intelligence and Manipulation 52

    Summarizing Emotional Intelligence 57

Chapter 2 59

The Benefits of Being Emotionally Intelligent 59

    The Importance of Emotional Intelligence 59

    Is It Possible That Emotional Intelligence Is Not Important? 69

    The Benefits of Emotional Intelligence 71

    The Emotional Intelligence and Conformity Debate .. 75

Chapter 3 79

Recognizing Your Own Emotions 79

    Recognizing Your Own Emotions as a Staging Ground
.... 85

    Self-Regulation Should Work in Concert with
Recognizing Your Emotions.. 89

    Activities That Can Improve Our Emotional State 91

Chapter 4.. 93

The Importance of Empathy 93

    The Skills of Empathy 100

Chapter 5.. 105

Building Solid Relationships 105

Chapter 6.. 113

Non-Verbal Communication 113

Chapter 7.. 119

Thirty Facts to Help You Be More Emotionally Intelligent
.... 119

Frequently Asked Questions.. 151

Conclusion 158

Introduction

Many people feel disconnected, causing them to seek methods of forming closer bonds to those around them. Modern methods of interconnecting can keep people in contact with those that matter to them, but interactions may seem brief, artificial, and lacking that closeness that empathy can provide. The bonds that come from truly relating to someone, from walking a day in their shoes as a character famously said in *To Kill A Mockingbird*, these ties cannot be underestimated as they stem from tapping into a potential that represents part of our legacy as human beings. This potential is called emotional intelligence, and it is a capability set that has been shown to be directly correlated with personal success.

Emotional intelligence can represent the dividing line between someone who experiences life through close connections and interactions with others and someone who simply lives. This capability can lead to a drastically improved quality of life as it can help men and women to infuse empathy into their lives. By having empathy for others, you can have more beneficial interactions as well as more positive outcomes in your own life, which can lead to happiness and personal success.

Emotional intelligence refers to the ability to recognize the feelings of others, to make distinctions between different emotions, and the ability to use emotions as a guide for behavior. It should come as no surprise that this quality first began to be appreciated in the 60s when people were starting to perceive the world through different tinted lenses. It took almost thirty years for the idea to enter common parlance and it has really taken off in the last 15 years. Emotional intelligence has come to the forefront in part as people have begun to recognize how disconnected they are from the world around them and to search for ways to rectify the situation.

There are many reasons why we as individuals may find ourselves in need of effective emotional intelligence. As society has arguably become faster-paced, more visually-oriented, and perhaps more superficial, human interactions, though brief, may become more significant. Men and women in the modern Western world may find that their lives are somehow less fulfilling than they were previously. Interactions with coworkers in the workplace or even with family members at home may feel stilted, strange, or dysfunctional.

Emotional intelligence, like everything else, is a two-way street. This is clear from the definitions that abound of the term. Most of these definitions recognize that a key component of emotional intelligence is not only recognizing the emotions of others but being able to gauge successfully your own emotions. As you will see as you delve further into this book, much of the changes that you can make in your life by being conscious of emotional intelligence and making changes based on it have to do with recognizing your own emotional state and the effect it has on your interactions with others.

Humans are social creatures, which means that understanding emotional intelligence and using it correctly is not only a boon but necessary. Something as simple as your facial expression, the position of your arms, how you are standing, and your eyes—all of these can be emotional indicators to others and can influence how others perceive you and the overall result of the interaction. Although no one can be expected to be conscious of every centimeter of their bodies at all times, by paying attention to the cues that we send others, we can not only have more beneficial interactions but also demonstrate empathy.

Many people may be reading this book because they are curious to learn how their lives can benefit from emotional intelligence, and much of that benefit comes from having empathy. One of the things that make human beings so special is that we are able to act altruistically—that is, we can perform actions that have no direct benefit to ourselves. This may include giving a donation of time or money to a cause that we care about, helping someone on the street, or giving a hand to someone at work even if it might be detrimental to ourselves. These are ways that we show others that we care and they are based on empathy.

Much has been said about the distinction between emotional intelligence and empathy, and the distinction is not always clear to people, even those that use these terms commonly. In truth, empathy is a critical component of emotional intelligence. In the last 20 years, many psychologists and others have attempted to create measures of emotional intelligence, and much of these measures really attempt to gauge is how empathic men and women are. Part of the difficulty in distinguishing between emotional intelligence and empathy stems from a general lack of understanding of empathy.

Empathy in part comes from successfully honing the twin abilities of correctly assessing another person's mental state based on their own subjective experience and showing compassion both within your own headspace and in interactions. Empathy, therefore, is a part of what is traditionally thought of as emotional intelligence, although empathy extends beyond merely having sympathy for others. Empathy requires also that we *have* empathy rather than merely show it. That is, that we experience the subjective emotions of others rather than merely relate to their experiences.

Emotional intelligence is often thought of as a distinct skill that individuals can acquire or hone. This is sometimes contrasted with empathy which some people are thought to have while others simply do not. Some readers may be familiar with the idea of the empath: a person who experiences the emotions and subjective experiences of others deeply. These empaths are thought to represent the idea of empathy being something intrinsic and particularly strong in certain people. Yet there is no reason why emotional intelligence should be a trainable skill while empathy is not. Indeed, with experience and training, people often become better at showing empathy because they get into the habit of trying to feel what others feel.

It is important not only to distinguish empathy from emotional intelligence but to distinguish empathy from the closely related sympathy. Sympathy is the ability to show tolerance and compassion, while empathy implies also that the individual relates to and experiences the feelings that the other person feels. Empathy, therefore, involves feeling sympathy for others while also experiencing their feelings. Honing emotional intelligence requires that you are skilled in empathy. As we will see in a moment, most models of emotional intelligence used by psychologists perceive empathy as being one of several skills that fall under the emotional intelligence umbrella.

Empathy is important because studies suggest that empathy can confer several benefits in our personal and professional lives, benefits that will be explored in this book. Studies have shown in particular that empathy is a critical skill in an effective leader. Leaders often have difficulty with demonstrating to their teams that they relate to them and that they care about their concerns. This leads to dissension within the group and lack of motivation. By showing empathy successfully, a leader can instill confidence in their leadership within the team while also pushing themselves towards success. This illustrates a unique way in which a leader can use empathy to interact with people on both a group and an individual level.

In this book, you will learn all that you ever wanted to know about the twin subjects of emotional intelligence and empathy. Your journey into the subject will begin by gaining a thorough idea of what emotional intelligence is and how it is measured. This is a topic that has been actively studied, and though this book does not approach the subject from the standpoint of a scientific review, it is important to understand all aspects of the term in order to, at the very least, be able to read further on the subject and converse with others from a position of knowledge.

It may seem like a foray off the beaten path, but no survey of emotional intelligence would be complete without an odyssey into human beings and their history. Sure, the subject of human evolution can be a can of worms, especially in countries like the United States where everyone seems to have a fixed opinion, but it is key to a thorough exploration of the subject to get an idea of why emotional intelligence is even something worth talking and writing about. Why did human beings develop empathy? Do other members of the animal kingdom demonstrate empathy? Are there people that do not demonstrate empathy at all or are unable to? These are all questions that are part and parcel of defining what emotional intelligence means to human beings.

Recognizing dysfunctional aspects of ourselves is important to getting the most out of life. Some people read books like the one you are reading now because they see that perhaps friends or others they know are successful and others are not, and they wonder what they can change to make their lives different. These are both perfectly acceptable reasons to try to learn more about emotional intelligence. Indeed there is no incorrect reason. Whatever your reason was to give this book a try, the significance of emotional intelligence will become clearer as you read on. The point will be driven home by providing you with examples of emotional intelligence so that you can recognize a side of the issue that may not have been clear before.

A key both to empathy and emotional intelligence is recognizing your own emotional state, which is not always as simple and straightforward as it sounds. This skill requires not only being conscious of how you are feeling from one moment to the next but also recognizing when your feelings are dysfunctional. There are many factors that influence how we perceive the world around us, many of them societal.

Therefore, we may not always recognize our dysfunctional thoughts and feelings as they may not necessarily be perceived as dysfunctional within society.

As stated above, empathy is really its own bag of worms because of difficulty some men and women have in understanding what precisely it means (and how it differs from other similar concepts like sympathy, emotional intelligence, and the like). But empathy is a skill that is most important to cognizant animals like human beings who must interact closely with one another. The fourth chapter of this book focuses on understanding empathy and infusing your life with it so that you may be more compassionate and tolerant in your daily life.

There are many ways that we can learn to be more emotionally aware or bring positivity into our lives. These adaptations may include meditation, discussing our thoughts and feelings with others, and generally making an effort to be more considerate of the feelings of others. One way that we can put emotional intelligence to good use is by focusing on relationships. It is easy to understand why relationships are important for success, but they are also important to live happy, contented, meaningful lives. Empathy seems to have limited use if we do not use it, right? Sure it is nice to be compassionate and tolerant in our minds, but we then have to use that in interactions, a skill that you will deal with here.

Non-verbal communication is very important in primates and like it or not, human beings are members of the primate family. Facial expressions, gestures, and other aspects of our appearance that indicate demeanor are key to indicating our perceptions to others. That means that others gauge our own emotional reactions to them by non-verbal communication. No discussion of emotional intelligence would be complete without a guide to non-verbal communication. In this book, you will learn to be conscious of the physical cues you are sending just as much as you're conscious of what you say and how you say it. Non-verbal communication, indeed, can make the difference between a compassionate, successful interaction and an unsuccessful one.

Learning about emotional intelligence and empathy would not get you very far if you were unable to translate those lessons into meaningful changes in your life. In the last chapter of the book, you will be able to easily synthesize all of the knowledge that you have learned using thirty simple facts. These facts are intended to help you connect the dots in terms of taking what you have read and bringing it into your own life. There is a reason why we often like to go to friends for advice or to bounce ideas off of. Sometimes we are not able to see the big picture, especially when it comes to ourselves. Equipped with these thirty tools, you can easily proceed step-by-step with real changes.

Emotional intelligence is not as hard as it seems. Human beings are naturally empathetic when it comes to the thoughts and feelings of others. Once you are able to understand how you like to be treated and how you feel when others are not empathetic towards you, you are already on the road to behaving towards others with emotional intelligence. This journey does not have to be like learning the steps of a chemical reaction in a chemistry textbook, indeed, it should not be. Your forays into utilizing emotional intelligence should be about behaving in a way that is positive and generates positive energy all around you. When all is said and done, that is what this book is all about.

Chapter 1

Emotional Intelligence Defined

The significance of interconnectivity is something that many men and women today find difficult to understand. Most people get up in the morning and go to work, they pay their bills, pay their taxes, get in touch with who it is they may need to get in touch with that day for whatever reason, and they come home and spend their time as they wish. Our life is easily compartmentalized and filled with matters of financial or pressing concern. Do I have enough money for this or that? Do I have time to do this thing or the other thing?

When we want something, we go to the supermarket and buy it with the money that we have earned from our jobs. There is no need for us to get into the uncomfortable situation of having to talk to someone to get the things we need. Indeed, nowadays, one need not even go to the supermarket, convenience store, shopping mall, or any other place where items are bought and sold. Everything is conveniently available online. If you do decide to pick up and move to a new city, you can pretty much guarantee that whatever company you are using to deliver things delivers there too. Not only do we as individuals not experience the feeling of being connected to particular people, but we also do not even experience what it feels like to be connected to a specific place.

Some of you who are reading this may originate outside of the Western world. Those of you that are from the Western world may have spent time in other places. Any of you who have ever lived in a "developing country" may get a sense of the difference here. If you live in a small village in Africa or Southeast Asia, you are unlikely to have an online service capable of delivering food and clothing to you as you would have in the United States. You may have to go to a local market and haggle for a fair price on a food item. On your way home from the market (walking of course), you may wave hello to your neighbor and they might offer you half of the melons that they got from their own venture to the market that day or perhaps some tomatoes from their garden.

Now, reading this, you may be wondering what the point of this discourse is. No, the point is not to convince you that modern, urban, commercialist society is "wrong" or "bad." The idea here is that modern society – a society in which we all move from one city to the next and can buy everything we need online without ever having to interact with anyone – is disconnecting. Humans naturally feel a connection to the land, like all other animals. This may seem unrelated to the discussion at hand, but it is actually an intrinsic part of it. By being connected to a specific place, we also become connected to the people that inhabit that place, people like ourselves.

Because men and women today are not connected to any place, and also because human interactions have often been reduced to business interactions or other interactions that have a specific purpose, we have all become disconnected. This means that not only is it oftentimes difficult for us to make emotional connections with others, but these emotional connections become more meaningful because they are rare or suddenly become more significant because the other person desperately needs an emotional connection.

If you find yourself having difficulty with empathy, you are not the only one. Lots of Americans today have a serious empathy concern. Homelessness, traumatized veterans of military campaigns, men and women who lose their jobs and are abandoned by their families, people facing substance abuse problems: these are all people who find themselves in a society and country where people have a problem feeling true empathy for another human being.

This empathy discussion does not mean that you open your house to someone who needs a place to stay or that you give things away haphazardly: that is not the point that you should take away from this initial discussion about empathy. The idea here is that various factors in society are contriving to make emotional intelligence a skill that many people do not have. Some people naturally seem to have empathy.

They start ahead of others when it comes to emotional intelligence for whatever reason. Most of us gain emotional intelligence by interacting with others, by caring about others, by seeing others as people who have lives, thoughts, and emotions similar to our own. What happens, therefore, when the number of meaningful interactions that we have with others is reduced by societal forces, or if people have difficulty interacting successfully because of television, movies, and the media?

In many Eastern religions, the idea of the interconnectivity of all mankind, even of all sentient species on the planet, is something that is assumed. We are interconnected by dent of being sentient animals that happen to live on a rock called the planet Earth. The intention of this chapter is not to proselytize or to convince you that your opinions on certain matters might be due for a change, but to illustrate why people today have an issue with emotional intelligence and why emotional intelligence suddenly seems more important now than ever before.

Many readers live lives that they know are dysfunctional in some ways. No one needs to tell you that you are having issues, you just sort of know. Sometimes these issues stem from a lack of emotional intelligence, or an inability to put basic emotional intelligence skills to good use. The way to begin your journey into removing your life dysfunctions, or even just improving your life if you prefer to look at it from that angle, is to understand that we are all interconnected. That is the first step. Once you understand that, you are ready to dive deeper into how science defines emotional intelligence so that you will be poised to use these skills effectively.

What Is Emotional Intelligence?

A major model of emotional intelligence views it as encompassing a variety of skills of which empathy is one. Emotional intelligence involves being conscious of one's own thoughts and feelings based on one's own internal state, being conscious of another person's emotional state based on their own personal experiences and internal concerns, demonstrating tolerance and compassion for others, and interacting with others in a way that demonstrates that you are conscious of their emotional state vis a vis your own.

Emotional intelligence is not merely an intellectual or social scientific term designed to muddy the waters as far as concepts that are obvious to people (as some of these terms do). Indeed, emotional intelligence seeks to do exactly the opposite. This term seeks to take something amorphous and transform it into a quality that has real value, one that people invest in and can measure. Of course, the idea of measuring something like emotional intelligence is a tricky one. Psychologists have attempted to create measures for emotional intelligence with the goal of making this concept similar to IQ, concrete skills (like spatial or computational skills), and the like. The idea here is that emotional intelligence is just as important to survival and to interactions as other skills are.

What makes emotional intelligence difficult for people to grasp is the nature of emotions. Emotions are imprecise things. They may change from one moment to the next, or we may fail to correctly read another's emotions or even our own. One of the takeaway concepts of this book will be how we can integrate certain concepts into our self-talk and our interactions in order to behave with more emotional intelligence, without necessarily being conscious of the other person's specific emotional state at that moment.

What do we mean by that? As we will explore later in the book, you can start with *empathy*, or what people commonly think of as empathy. Many men and women think of tolerance and caring compassion as empathy, and this is certainly one component of the word. By showing compassion for others, we can use emotional intelligence even if we do not know what the other person is feeling. There are things that you can say to a person during an interaction that demonstrate that you are listening and that you relate to them. Empathy is more than the ability to show tolerance and compassion. An intrinsic component of empathy is the capability of relating to another person and feeling what they feel. This will all be explained in the chapter dealing with empathy.

Before we delve more deeply into the specific emotional intelligence skills that you will be learning in this book, it is a good idea to start approaching emotional intelligence scientifically. This is one of those things that can be a good thing or it can be a bad thing. Although psychologists have attempted to take empathy out of the realm of hippies and psychedelic drug users (joking, of course) by clearly defining, categorizing it, and finding ways to measure it, what this scientific approach does is open empathy up for a little bit of denaturing for lack of a better word. Empathy is not a frog that you can dissect to learn how the central nervous system works. In order to use empathy effectively, you have to learn to understand all of its aspects while still treating it as the soul-filled, energy-infused concept that it is.

In other words, emotional intelligence may benefit from a little bit of a hard science approach. With that said, the reader should still try to approach emotional intelligence as a quality that is not quite the same as becoming a black belt in karate or learning to write code. So caveat out of the way, let us start by breaking down that concept so closely related to emotional intelligence – empathy – as an important part of defining and understanding what emotional intelligence truly signifies. Empathy can be broken down into the three following components:

- Accuracy
- Compassion
- Interactions

What this means is that empathy is more than just caring about others or demonstrating that you care about others. Empathy also technically requires that one is able to understand others accurately. This is where the relationship with emotional intelligence begins to be significant. Because emotional intelligence for many represents a way to quantify empathy, the accuracy element of empathy becomes something that psychologists are able to predict as a way of indicating where a particular individual's emotional intelligence skills lie.

The History of the Study of Emotional Intelligence and Different Models

Emotional intelligence appeared as a term in the mid-1960s. A 1966 paper in a child psychiatry journal examined the new concept from the standpoint of a therapeutic approach. The concept mulled around a bit until the 80s when it reappeared as social scientists began to look at intelligence differently. They were attempting to define intelligence differently than it had been before in order to take full stock of human capability. Intelligence has always been a sticky subject to define, and the issue of IQ testing is one that has always been controversial.

New definitions of intelligence from this period advocated for the idea of multiple intelligences—that is, abilities that focused not on what was thought of as cognitive abilities but on the ability to interact with others and understand one's own internal emotional state. The multiple intelligences defined included both intrapersonal intelligence and interpersonal intelligence. Intrapersonal intelligence referred to the ability to accurately understand one's own motivations, thoughts, and feelings. Interpersonal intelligence referred to the ability to accomplish the same with others.

These definitions were all a part of redefining intelligence, an endeavor that continues to this day. It is a bit ironic that in their attempt to move away from defining traditional intelligence with IQ tests and other measures, social scientists came up with models of emotional intelligence that attempted to quantify this quality with its own tests and measures. Indeed, early on in the history of emotional intelligence as an academic subject, social scientists referred to this quality as EQ, or emotional quotient, a designation that continues to this day in many articles and books.

In spite of the increasing scholarly activity around emotional intelligence and emotional quotient (or EQ), the term did not begin to enter common parlance until the mid-90s when a popular book introduced the term to the average reader. The book was entitled *Emotional Intelligence – Why It Can Matter More Than IQ*, and it was written in 1995, which really was perfect timing considering that this was really when people were beginning to take a hard look at IQ testing. Talk shows, nightly news reports, and the experiences that many parents had with schools had made IQ a subject of distaste and suspicion in many people's minds. The idea that there was a type of intelligence that not only could not be measured by standard tests currently available but was actually more important seemed too good to be true.

Emotional intelligence has not been overhyped. Studies have suggested that people who demonstrate higher than normal emotional intelligence find success in their personal relationships, careers, and leadership roles. These findings have been controversial through the years and research has amped up in recent years to better understand these benefits. One of the results of all the interest around emotional intelligence has been the development of alternative models to try to define the concept better and put it to practical use.

The three common models all attempt to categorize emotional intelligence with the end goal of quantifying it. Several tests and measures have been created to measure the variables established in the three main models. Those models are as follows:

- The Mixed Model
- The Ability Model
- The Trait Model

The Mixed Model attempts to define emotional intelligence in terms of emotional competencies: skills that develop over time and which can be improved with dedication. These emotional competencies encompass the range of what many social scientists consider empathy but stretch beyond them. These emotional competencies include motivation, self-regulation, self-awareness, empathy, and social skill. An important component of this approach to emotional intelligence is the idea of self regulation, which includes shifting or halting one's own dysfunctional thoughts and emotions. Empathy often focuses on active skills that show caring, but being able to control one's own emotions is important regardless of which model speaks most to the reader.

The Ability Model approaches emotional intelligence from the standpoint of a skill that can be honed to create meaningful interactions. Although all models accept the importance of emotional intelligence in social interactions, the ability model takes a practical approach, seeing this range of capacities as something that has a clear use. According to this model, emotional intelligence is used to perceive, understand, manage, and use practically emotions. These are perceived as four distinct abilities that comprise emotional intelligence. One advantage of this model is that it approaches the subject simply with terms that do not need further explanation. Like other models of emotional intelligence, measures have been created to allow psychologists and other social scientists to measure this spectrum of capabilities.

The Trait Model is distinct from the other two as it focuses on an individual's self-report about their emotional abilities. This model evolved later than the others and recognizes the difficulties that come from measuring emotional ability, even with carefully-crafted standard measures. By focusing on self-report, this model makes emotional ability a quantity closely tied to personality. This model takes the assumptions made by the ability but makes emotional intelligence a personality trait that is distinct from cognitive ability.

Although these models may seem peripheral to the discussion of emotional intelligence used as a practical set of skills in this book, it is important to note that the role of emotional intelligence vis a vis "traditional" cognitive ability is still a subject of discussion. It would seem that emotional intelligence should be in a realm of its own, distinct from cognitive ability, but there does seem to be a tacit assumption in these models that emotional intelligence (EQ) needs to prove itself before being taken seriously.

Controversy Surrounding Emotional Intelligence

Perhaps the biggest problem surrounding emotional intelligence is whether or not it should be called "intelligence." Much scholarly debate has revolved around whether emotional intelligence should be construed as a type of intelligence, which the earliest researchers in the field assumed. They saw emotional intelligence as a skill that was similar to cognition as measured by IQ tests. Detractors of this view posit that emotional capabilities represent rather the ability to use intelligence to perceive and interact with others from an emotional standpoint. It is not in itself a type of intelligence.

The subject is charged as there seems to have been from the beginning to place emotional intelligence on a level with other accepted forms of intelligence, even in the face of difficulty measuring emotional intelligence accurately. Some suppose that emotional intelligence should not be considered as intelligence as it cannot, in fact, be measured effectively and accurately. Indeed, the self-reporting used in the mixed model has been criticized as it may incline the user to report information inaccurately in order to alter the results.

The Role of Emotional Intelligence

Human beings are primates, which mean that we naturally live in social groups in which constant interactions are critical. As primates, we learn our role in the group through these interactions. This system allows the social group to function as each individual knows their place in groupings that are frequently hierarchical. Emotional intelligence allows individuals to correctly assess their interactions with others and consequently their place within the social group.

There are a number of reasons why being able to assess the emotions of others is important. This critical skill, of accurately understanding the emotional state of others and reacting in an appropriate way, allowed individuals to correctly assess danger while at the same time estimating goodwill. Being able to assess danger allowed our early ancestors to respond in ways to protect themselves by getting out of danger. Being able to estimate goodwill by a similar token allowed our ancestors to form alliances, create long-lasting friendships, and perhaps even attract or maintain potential mates.

As human beings living in a modern time, we are very far removed from the sorts of lives that our early primate ancestors lived, or at least it seems this way. It may not seem obvious why being able to assess danger or goodwill is important today in the same way that it was tens of thousands of years ago. We take for granted that we live in a society ostensibly constructed of law and order, good government, and goodwill between the individuals within the society.

In reality, these abilities to be able to determine ill will or goodwill using emotions is still important today, and people still use it often without knowing. Things that people say to us or even their facial expressions clue us in on whether or not the other person "likes us" or "doesn't like us." Most people normally adjust their own behavior based on these perceptions that ultimately stem from emotional intelligence. We may choose not to work with a person we think dislikes us or to avoid them (rightly or wrongly), or we may choose to befriend and seek companionship with someone that we believe likes us.

As a way of understanding emotional intelligence in the context of human behavior in evolution, it is important to analyze the example of adjusting our own behavior based on a perception of like and dislike. Think about what happens in this interaction. The person that you are talking to may smile at you or appear glad to see you (indicating like), or they may frown or seem disturbed at your sudden arrival, indicating dislike. But, as simple as this interaction may seem, it is based on a number of assumptions that are impacted by the respective emotional intelligence of the players involved.

For example, someone may frown or appear irritated at your appearance because they are already late for a meeting or they are having a bad day. This gesture of theirs (a particular facial expression or short words) may have little or nothing to do with how they feel about you overall. This means that it is important for you to use your emotional intelligence to interpret what is actually going on in this situation. In other words, if you assume that particular gestures indicate dislike, then you would be forgoing a potentially mutual beneficial interaction because of an inaccurate assessment of the other person's emotions.

This example should illustrate why the aforementioned emotional intelligence models approach the subject of emotional intelligence in the way that they do. Although the models differ in some important ways, they see emotional intelligence as a skill that can be acquired and honed; these models also see correctly understanding another's emotions as well as your own as important. Therefore, successful emotional intelligence skills are more than just being sensitive to another's emotional state. An essential aspect of emotional intelligence is *accuracy*.

It can be argued that successful emotional intelligence skills are essential to human beings in a civilized state. For primates swinging from trees or hanging around a watering hole, it may matter less whether or not you successfully assess someone's like or dislike compared to people that live within a civilization. For example, a primate (or early human ancestor in this example) may estimate that the other primate at the watering hole dislikes them. So what do they do? Well, if they are a chimpanzee or gorilla they might attack, or they might simply move to another watering hole.

But the significance of emotional intelligence (applied correctly) in this interaction is greater for human primates living in complex societies where the individuals are constantly in close proximity with one another. Societies cannot function well if individuals are constantly (and inaccurately) perceiving danger and reacting accordingly. Indeed, this tendency to inaccurately perceive danger may be increasing in modern society where we are constantly being exposed to triggering influences from television news, social media, and other sources.

Emotional Intelligence and Resilience

In a second, we will delve more deeply into the subject of problems that people in modern society may be having with their collective emotional intelligence skills, but before we get there, it is important to meander into the idea of resilience. At first glance, it may not seem obvious how emotional intelligence is related to resilience. Resilience refers to the ability of an individual to handle stress, change, or other disturbing factors. Individuals may be naturally resilient or they may become more resilient over time because of life events that strengthen this quality in them. Conversely, individuals may also become less resilient if they allow stressors or life changes to weaken them and their ability to handle additional stressors in the future.

Emotional intelligence comes into play in the realm of resilience because emotional intelligence skills may cause us to be more resilient than others who do not use these skills appropriately (or are lacking them). Let us meander back to our example of the person who perceived dislike because the person they were speaking to frowned when they were approaching them. Although the frown (or other negative gesture) is an indicator of another person's mental state, this indicator needs to be interpreted correctly in order to actually be meaningful. Someone that is always interpreting negative gestures as pertaining to them personally may become less resilient or more stressed because they constantly perceive themselves as being under attack.

On the other hand, the individual who is able to take a step back and say: "This person appears disturbed right now, I hope they are alright," this person is using emotional intelligence skills and therefore is able to reduce the subjective import of minor cues within interactions. In other words, a person who correctly realizes that there are many reasons why someone may appear upset or angry and does not automatically assume that it has something to do with them will not always assume danger and therefore will not react in a way that suggests danger (and may actually create a dangerous situation or worsen one).

By this thinking, a person that uses emotional intelligence to correctly assess another's mental or emotional state can become more resilient because they are not reacting to cues that may have an ambiguous meaning. Think about these sorts of cues as an object being thrown in your direction. A person who is able to say: "This object was not meant for me, I am going to keep moving," will become more resilient than a person who sees every object thrown in their direction as meant for themselves and reacts to everyone.

It is important to point out here that no one is expected to have this sort of emotional intelligence skill from the moment we are born. Indeed, this sort of skill (of using emotional intelligence to become more resilient) will naturally be increased and improved over time as we have more meaningful interactions with other people and learn to understand both ourselves and others better.

Not Allowing Another's Mental State to Impact Your Own

An important coping mechanism in psychology (and a successful strategy for achieving a happy and successful life) is the idea of not allowing the internal states of others to affect our own internal states. This is related to the ideas of resilience mentioned above, in which we responded appropriately to others without reacting to perceived negativity, but it is a distinct skill or coping strategy. In the example above, we were able to correctly assess that the individual was not angry with us even though they appeared to be, but what if the person was angry?

This idea of not reacting to others in a negative way expounds on the basic tenets of emotional intelligence although it too is a distinct skill. There will be times when others are angry with us or dislike us. Does that mean that we should respond to this anger or dislike by being angry and disliking them too in turn? This is certainly something that we could do and that some would do, but this can become dysfunctional for ourselves and lead to us becoming less resilient. Remember, resilience is the ability to handle life's challenges and stressors, and people who are constantly in a state of reacting negatively to perceived negativity from others will be less resilient than others who do not respond this way.

Therefore, resilience can be improved by using emotional intelligence not only to accurately assess others but to control or change our own internal states. It is natural to react to others, but as mentioned above, this can become dysfunctional. Although it may be a natural reaction to respond to the dislike of others with our own dislike, by not reacting in this way, we can diffuse a situation and become happier. This is not only a coping strategy, but it is an effective use of emotional intelligence. Recall that the mixed model specifically mentions self-regulation as a skill that falls within the overall grouping of emotional intelligence skills.

Self-regulation thus becomes not only an example of emotional intelligence applied to everyday situations, but an actual coping strategy that is regarded by many psychologists as among the most important coping strategies that people can use in their lives. Self-regulation means that you can successfully understand and halt your own emotions. In doing this, you not only use emotional intelligence and improve outcomes in your own life, but you may actually turn a negative reaction with another person into a positive one.

For example, you may say to yourself: "This person is angry, they are probably having a bad day so I should be sympathetic." Or: "This person is angry, let me offer them some words of encouragement or give them a compliment." This allows you to create something positive out of something negative. Although it may not be our first reaction to respond to negativity with positivity, this does allow us to be more emotionally intelligent and to create better social interactions for ourselves as well as others.

Societal Problems with Emotional Intelligence

Much has been written about how technological and environmental changes have altered the way that we interact with one another. It may not seem obvious to many people living today, but it was not long ago that people were living in rural areas, on farms, in villages, or in other places that were not in cities. Men and women had meaningful interactions with one another and were able to be more positive and genial (arguably) because they understood the people around them due to constant exposure and familiarity.

Think about what happens when people began to move away from small rural communities and no longer understood or could accurately predict the emotional states of other people because they were unfamiliar with them. Exposure breeds familiarity. As people moved to places where they were unfamiliar with others (the typical scenario in many large urban areas of today), it became more difficult for people to accurately assess the emotional states of others.

Although it is unlikely that the current trends of living will ever be reversed (it is arguable that they need to be), people can still have positive and meaningful interactions with others by thinking about putting the skills that we have begun to list to good use. Again, this is not merely a matter of accurately understanding the emotions of others or even your own. You also must be able to alter your own emotions in order to improve your own internal state and diffuse potentially heated situations.

When we refer to societal problems with emotional intelligence, what we really mean is that environmental factors have caused interactions with people to become more charged, a reality which may be obvious to many readers. The times where people say hello to one another on the street or stop for a friendly chat is long past for many. Today, we do not know many of the people that we pass on the street and we also do not know what their intentions are.

But approaching our interactions from the

standpoints of accurate understanding and self-regulation allows us to infuse positivity into environments that in many ways have become negative. Individuals may be accused of being negative by others, which can lead to hurt as they may not perceive themselves as being negative. Many "negative" people simply have been hurt before or have been reared in threatening environments causing them to appear unsettled or disturbed merely out of habits.

Someone who is not compassionate or empathetic may perceive people like this negatively and may be inclined to behave with negative actions toward them. Although we may not like it, this tendency to act negatively towards people that are disliked is a part of human nature. But emotional intelligence allows us to act outside the constraints of what is really animal nature and to behave more humanely towards others. It is actually animal nature, not human nature, that causes men and women to attack others (whether verbally, through slander, or physically) based on our negative perceptions of others.

There is a saying that may be helpful to illustrate this point. The saying goes: "Human beings are 90 percent animal and 10 percent human." Although the meaning of the saying may not be clear to some readers at first, it really underscores this idea that many of our natural ways of interacting with one another represent our animal origins and not our capabilities of human beings. As human beings, we are capable of independent action and thought. This means that we are capable of acting based on our own choices rather than on impulses that stem from our animal nature.

Emotional intelligence, therefore, can represent our ability to behave with human qualities rather than with animal nature. Emotional intelligence *can* do this, but it does not necessarily always do this as we will see shortly. In the next chapter, we will illustrate this point by going into examples of emotional intelligence used effectively and ineffectively. But before we get there, we do need to talk about one controversy surrounding emotional intelligence. We cover that in this chapter because it is part of the basic definition of emotional intelligence that falls within the scope of this chapter.

Emotional Intelligence and Manipulation

Most books that deal with subjects that are being promoted or encouraged tend to stray away from aspects of the subject that are controversial or that may incline the reader to stray away from the idea. But the purpose of this book is to give you a complete understanding of emotional intelligence, and that includes understanding why some people are not advocates of it. In order to truly adopt a thing and believe in it, you need to know the pros and cos.

In the psychological and social scientific fields, there is controversy about whether emotional intelligence should be considered intelligence, or even if it should be considered a beneficial skill at all. Although different social scientists have their reasons for why they support or do not support emotional intelligence, the idea of emotional intelligence being used as a tool of manipulation is a major source for detractors.

The idea here is that emotional intelligence can be used to manipulate others with the goal of the manipulator achieving their specific ends. What this means in the case of emotional intelligence is that the person utilizing emotional intelligence assesses the internal state of the other person accurately and effectively. They then use this knowledge that they have gained (for it is a type of knowledge) to alter their own thoughts and behaviors but not in order to have just a positive interaction or a positive outcome. They would use their skill and the resulting information gained to alter the other person's thoughts or beliefs.

Manipulation is the tactic of altering the thoughts and behaviors of others. It should not be difficult to understand how emotional intelligence would be useful here. Emotional intelligence allows you to accurately gauge the thoughts of others based on what they have said or on their behaviors. An effective manipulator would therefore require some level of emotional intelligence to be able to manipulate well. If they were not able to accurately gauge the thoughts and emotions of others, then their manipulations would fail because they would be based on false information.

In this example, emotional intelligence would be distinct from empathy. As is obvious in this scenario, the manipulator is not acting with compassion or tolerance towards the other, and if they are, it is for reasons that have little to do with the other person. In this case, the manipulator is using only a type of emotional intelligence (or some emotional intelligence capabilities) with the goal of manipulation. Therefore, the stereotypical example of the manipulator would be of a person who has some emotional intelligence skills (perhaps even great emotional intelligence skills) but is not fully using emotional intelligence because they are leaving out the empathy here.

But (and there is an important but here) manipulation itself is not straightforward as it first appears. Manipulation is a term that is charged with a fair measure of negativity because people perceive it as a tactic utilized to cause them to act outside their own desires or intentions. Manipulation, in fact, overlaps with persuasion. Indeed, some people use the term persuasion when they wish to advocate for manipulation but do not wish to engender any of the negative connotations that people commonly have with manipulation.

Persuasion is similar to manipulation in that it also involves the capability to change the thoughts or opinions of others. Many people see manipulation as being expressly used for malign purposes, but some have argued that manipulation and persuasion are one and the same. When you persuade one, you are attempting to change their thoughts and behaviors, and the reason why may only be known to you. In reality, you may be persuading for a negative design just as a so-called manipulator does.

Manipulation can be used to change people's thoughts, opinions, and behaviors in a way beneficial to themselves. Manipulation does not have to be used for sinister design. Some people "manipulate" their loved ones into going out more or going on a blind date because they want them to be happier. Some people "manipulate" people they know into accepting a job that they believe will be beneficial for them by putting their talents to good use. Although these examples are more on the manipulation end than the persuasion end, the goals are not sinister.

The point here is that saying that emotional intelligence is not necessarily beneficial because it can be used for manipulation is arguably not a strong charge against emotional intelligence. This position is based on an inaccurate assessment of manipulation, one that assumes that manipulation is always used with a malicious design. If manipulation based on emotional intelligence is used for positivity, then the emotional intelligence that it is based on also has a positive use.

Summarizing Emotional Intelligence

At this point, you should have an understanding of emotional intelligence. Extending beyond the ability to accurately understand the emotions of yourself and to others, extending also beyond showing the tolerance and compassion that constitute empathy, emotional intelligence also includes a wide range of skills that includes self-regulation. By changing or halting your own dysfunctional thoughts, you can improve your interactions with others for the benefit of you both. Emotional intelligence can also make you more resilient.

Although emotional intelligence and empathy are often confused and conflated, many in the psychological field perceive empathy as a type of emotional intelligence or a skill that falls under the umbrella of emotional intelligence. Empathy essentially refers to the act of understanding the emotional state of others and responding with compassion and tolerance. There are different models of emotional intelligence, and one of the more prominent models posits that emotional intelligence is made up of several intelligences that can be learned and honed, including empathy.

Though there is a debate about whether emotional intelligence is a type of intelligence like cognitive reasoning, or if it is merely a skill or a set of skills, the benefits of emotional intelligence should be clear to most readers. Emotional intelligence allowed us as individuals to accurately assess the emotions, desires, and intentions of others in order to survive. Emotional intelligence has become more challenging due to various societal factors, but this only means that these skills are more important now than ever. In the next chapter, you will understand even more about emotional intelligence in order to begin the process of learning how to use it effectively.

Chapter 2

The Benefits of Being Emotionally Intelligent

The Importance of Emotional Intelligence

One of the most enduring stories of life in the United States takes place in a small town in Alabama, as penned by Harper Lee. *To Kill A Mockingbird* is standard teaching in many schools across the United States because it deals with issues that impacted Americans in the early 19th century but which still affect us today. In *To Kill A Mockingbird*, one of the characters says (to paraphrase) that a person can never be really understood until you walk a day in their shoes. That adage has become a common phrase that people use in parlance but it illustrates how important empathy, and by extension, emotional intelligence, can be in creating communities where individuals understand one another and are able to work well together.

You do not have to live in Monroeville, Alabama to understand the importance of emotional intelligence. It was Harper Lee's experiences living in this town in the 1930s that helped her create the images of the town of Macomb that are stilled burned into the minds of people who read the book years ago. Even in seemingly close-knit communities, members can suffer from problems identifying or interacting with one another. But as Atticus Finch says in the book, we never really understand people until we view the world through their eyes.

It goes without saying that relating to others can be difficult sometimes, that is why empathy and emotional intelligence are such critical skills, especially for leaders. Many of us come from different cultural backgrounds, have different age demographics, different interests, or have a host of other things about us that make us singular, but we still have to be able to relate to one another on some functional level in order to live together. We do not have to be as starkly different as some of the characters and groups in *To Kill A Mockingbird* are in order to illustrate the point of the importance of empathy. Even within close-knit groups of people who may seem similar, albeit on the surface, people can still experience the seemingly insurmountable task of relating to and experiencing another's experiences.

This may lead some to think that life would be a lot easier if we were all the same, and this is something that some people have suggested as ways that human beings might progress in the future. Some scientists claim that they can eliminate suffering by modifying genes to remove birth defects, allergies, illnesses, dwarfism or other causes of short heights. What is next? Eliminating genes that cause people to be too tall or bad at music? One could argue that it is these differences among people that make life interesting and exciting. If people were all the same, then artists and poets would have no inspiration. It would be hard to pen a poem about a beautiful woman if all women looked exactly the same. Every poet has their own idea of the sort of person, or even the sort of object, that inspires them.

The point here is that differences should not be perceived as an obstacle that needs to be overcome by emotional intelligence. Studies suggest that good leaders use empathy to relate to people that have different skill backgrounds, hail from different parts of the world, or otherwise distinguishable from others the leaders typically work with. Does this mean that leaders should only hire certain types of people? No. Studies also show that diverse workforces lead to innovation and resilience as a diverse group is capable of coming up with a diverse set of ideas that may prove beneficial to a company. Therefore, if you are approaching the subject of emotional intelligence from the standpoint of improving leadership capabilities or another workplace skillset, keep in mind that being able to empathize with people makes you a better leader and ultimately benefits your organization.

In fact, empathy is regarded as so important to

company dynamics that some organizations have begun to pen empathy manuals or guides to help their employees learn to be more empathetic. As we have established, emotional intelligence is not merely something that you are born with and that is it: the end of the story. Emotional intelligence can be learned. Team leaders can train for emotional intelligence and coach it with regular training initiatives. Although this may seem like devoting time toward something that provides minimal (albeit some) benefit to an organization, the potential benefits are actually so great that it is difficult to accurately measure them.

Studies show that 50% of managers are rated poorly by their employees. It is believed that much of this poor assessment of leadership by staff stems, at least in part, from a lack of emotional intelligence shown by leadership. There is a saying, People may not remember what you said to them, but they will remember how you made them feel. Leaders who are able to show active empathy engender the support, confidence, and respect of their employees and peers alike. Remember, empathy is not merely just sympathy—that is, demonstrating tolerance and compassion.

The key here is to have empathy: to truly feel what another is feeling. The mother who is dealing with a sick child and is distressed. The father who is working multiple jobs to make ends meet and still cannot keep his head above water. Being a leader means truly jumping into another's skin and relating to them. You do not want to be the manager who fires that aforementioned father for a minor infraction. This will not only adversely impact the individual who is fired, but it also impacts how your employees perceive you: as someone who lacks empathy for others.

We can drive the point home further by pointing out that others can generally tell when someone is being genuine with them or not. You may demonstrate being sympathetic for others through your words and gestures, which is important, but if you do not actually have empathy within yourself, then it will show. This exercise is not as difficult as it may seem to some people. This is not about putting on a show.

Having empathy is as simple as thinking that just as you would want someone to relate to you when you are going through a difficult time, by the same token you should learn to relate to others when they are going through their own troubles.

Of course, part of the problem here is that life does not always dole out the hard times equally. Some people may have difficulty feeling empathy because they have not had many struggles in their own lives. People in the United States often do not feel sympathy for the homeless because they make assumptions about who homeless people are and why they are homeless. It can be difficult for people to really walk in another's shoes when they actually have not walked in their shoes. But if you remember that life can change in an instant and that your own circumstances may change, it may help you to see that others going through hard times really are not that diffcrent from you.

The purpose of this chapter is not to inundate the reader with quotes and adages, but there is another quote that is meaningful here. The adage goes that we should be compassionate to others because one day we may need someone to be compassionate to us. As was stressed in the first chapter, human beings are interconnected by virtue of being members of the same species, by dent of living on the same planet, and simply by having a natural tendency to seek companionship and close relations with others, whether through romantic relationships, friendships, or other forms. By showing empathy, we not only infuse our lives with positivity, but we help to encourage empathy in others.

Going back to the point of empathy as a critical leadership skill, by demonstrating empathic behaviors in their management capacity, a leader also sets the stage for their own employees demonstrating empathy when they go on to become managers. Some individuals reading this may be managers in their organizations. You may be thinking that an organization where everyone is super-sensitive and obsessed with emotions and feelings will be an organization where work is not being performed. Studies suggest that leaders showing empathy perform betters than leaders that do not. Workers will be more motivated to work for an employer that perceives them as a valued member of the team rather than just another warm body in the assembly line.

It may help future and present leaders to use the analogy of the leader as a king and his or her team as the subjects. Subjects that are dissatisfied with the king or feel that the king is unconcerned with them rebel or they do not support the king when the king turns to them for support. Louis XIV of France famously said, "I am the state," and he may have meant that power in the kingdom was concentrated in his own person, but he also made the statement that the king was somehow intrinsically connected with the collective achievement of both the people and the kingdom.

This was illustrated all too well when, almost 80 years after the death of Louis XIV, the people of Paris stormed the Bastille and began the French Revolution, one of the most important events in world history. The French Revolution set the stage for the political and social changes that have created the world that we live in. If it were not for the French Revolution, men and women in the Western world might still be paying feudal dues to their lords and being excluded from any expression of political or personal power.

By failing to have empathy for their people, the kings of France became alienated from them, which caused the people to see the kings as being responsible for their sufferings (which they were, at least in part). There is a film called *Jefferson In Paris* that demonstrated how little empathy the wealthy elites of France had for the peasants that toiled the land and generated the wealth that the peasants spent. In this scene, a noble couple had a fancy dinner and it becomes warm in the dining room. They tell the servants to smash the windows to let the air in because the windows were designed to not be opened. The windows that were smashed would be replaced. Whenever the couple entertained and the temperature grew to warm, the windows were smashed only to be replaced the next day. All of which was paid for by peasants who could not feed their children.

This is an extreme example of a society where there is no empathy, or at least where a segment of the population feels no empathy for the other. It is frightening to think that our own society moves in this similar direction, especially in a country like the United States that was intended to represent a set of rights designed to engender personal freedom and to resist tyrannical institutions. Leaving aside the discussion of whether or not the United States has succeeded or failed in this design, if we all took the time to have empathy for one another, we could create better work environments, better home environments, and improved relationships.

Is It Possible That Emotional Intelligence Is Not Important?

A lot of the controversy surrounding emotional intelligence revolves around whether or not emotional intelligence is what it purports to be. The three different models approach the concept differently, but generally see emotional intelligence as *intelligence* or, at the very least, a set of capabilities that represent a distinct skill. Detractors of this view suggest that emotional intelligence does not represent a distinct ability. They perceive emotional intelligence as a construct that has little meaningful value outside the realm of discussion and politics.

In this view, emotional intelligence is a cognition that has been applied to emotions. In other words, emotional intelligence is really just applying one's ability to assess and understand the emotions of one and others. A suggestion that this might be true lies in the definition of emotional intelligence as well as the fact that emotional intelligence can often easily be learned by people that have problems with it. The definitions of emotional intelligence typically use the terms assessing, understanding, and the like, which represent basics forms of cognition. The only difference is that these forms of cognition have been applied to emotions.

But this interpretation of emotional intelligence – as merely a type of cognition and not as something distinct and important – fails to take account of empathy. Cognition does not include the ability to feel another person's emotions or to be able to connect with them in an emotional way without words, sometimes even not really understanding why you have an emotional connection. Some people cry when they see another person cry These empaths may feel sadness or pain merely by being in close proximity to someone feeling these things. These realities have nothing to do with cognition—that is, the brain processing information with a specific goal in mind. Empaths seemed to be cued into the emotional world in a way that even psychologists have difficulty understanding.

The Benefits of Emotional Intelligence

The benefits of emotional intelligence to leaders are clear. Many studies have shown that organizations can benefit from emotional intelligence training. Also, leaders who demonstrate empathy are rated bated by their employees and perform better on many measures of job performance. But what about outside the realm of management? There has been much study on the subject of possible benefits emotional intelligence can have on individuals. Much of these take the form of meta-analyses or reviews that synthesize the data from multiple studies to get a better picture of the practical uses of emotional intelligence and empathy.

What these studies have found should not come as a surprise to those who have cultivated emotional intelligence and understand how it can cause change. Below is a list of some of the benefits of emotional intelligence that have been studied.

- Improved psychological satisfaction: Individuals who use emotional intelligence show more self-esteem, are more satisfied with life, and are often free of the anxiety and depression that plagues others.

- Better health choices: Research has shown that emotional intelligence is correlated negatively with bad health decisions and dangerous health behaviors. Therefore, those with low emotional intelligence tend to make these bad choices and engage in risky behaviors.

- Improved academic performance: Studies suggest that highly emotionally intelligent people perform better in academics as rated by their teachers.

- Improved social interactions in business settings: Some research has suggested that highly emotionally intelligent people are better at negotiating deals and in situations of social dynamics in general in the workplace.

- Better perception by peers: People who cultivate emotional intelligence are perceived in a more positive way than those with less emotional intelligence. This has been shown to include perceptions of social skills and geniality.

- Improved personal and romantic relationships: High emotional intelligence has been found to be correlated with more successful intimate relationships and relationships with family members.

- Generally improved social interactions: Much of emotional intelligence measurement and assessment comes from reports by individuals and others. These assessments find that high emotional intelligence is correlated with better social skills, better relationships with others, and more pacific relationships and less conflict.

- Better relationship outcomes in children: Emotional intelligence has been shown to be very important and highly beneficial in children. Children with high emotional intelligence engage in fewer antisocial behaviors, have better relationships with other children, and adhere more closely to the norms and mores of society.

It is not possible to list all of the benefits of empathy and emotional intelligence, but studies performed on the subject do seem to strike a pattern. These studies suggest that, in general, those with high emotional intelligence are more successful across all measures of perception by others and in relationships than their peers with lower abilities in this area. This goes back to what we were saying before about interconnectivity. Because we are all connected as individuals, those who are able to assess the perceptions of others well tend to get along better in a group than those who do not. This is shown in the list of benefits above.

The Emotional Intelligence and Conformity Debate

This discussion of the benefits of emotional intelligence taken as a whole is a natural segue into another important debate on the subject, the subject of conformity. Conformity is an issue to address within the scope of this book for a number of reasons. Bullying incidents have become a major topic in the United States because of highly publicized incidents both in the setting of school and outside of it. Bullying happens both because the bully lacks emotional intelligence, but also because (as some studies suggest) the victim may be less sensitive to cues that are being presented by others and the bully finds an opportunity.

This is a controversial subject because some of the emotional intelligence data around bullying suggest that victims of bullying would be more successful in interpersonal relationships if they conform. Although that does seem to be the line in much of the research on the subject (even if it is implicit), that is not the line taken by this work. When all is said and done, it is the bully who chooses to attack their victim because they see an opportunity. Usually, the victim of bullying is someone who is perceived as weak or vulnerable, often because they have been ostracized by the group or they are an outsider of some kind.

The data around the benefits of emotional intelligence focus a lot on interpersonal relationships.

People with high emotional intelligence tend to have better or more successful relationships with others. This has caused some to suggest that emotional intelligence merely leads to individuals conforming with social norms or group demands. Although it is not easy to refute this assessment of the emotional intelligence and conformity debate, it is clear that if individuals showed empathy rather than merely conformity, then incidents of bullying will be reduced.

There is unlikely to ever be a time where we are all so similar to one another that bullying does not occur. That is unless, scientists decide that all human beings should come from test tubes and all the individual characteristics of people should be muted, which unfortunately is a distinct possibility. As long as we are different, we will have to deal with bullying. But by encouraging empathy in the workplace and in school, we can improve what the end result of bullying is. We may not always be able to prevent a bully from seizing the opportunity that a weak victim presents, but we can instill empathy in those in the social group, leading them to come to the aid of someone being bullied rather than joining in as often happens.

Chapter 3

Recognizing Your Own Emotions

Assessing your own emotional state is a key step in honing emotional intelligence as well as having empathy in general. Some people may be constantly cued in to their emotional states while some others may go a day or a week without thinking about it at all. Although it may be easy to fall into the trap of generalizations on the subject of the sort of people who think about their emotions and those that do not, the issue is not as straightforward as it may at first seem.

People who report that they think about their emotions frequently may be characterized as the sensitive, empathic sort. These are the sorts of people who naturally ask others how they are feeling, or who give others encouragement when they hear news that suggests that the other may be going through a trying time. Some people naturally recognize their own emotional state and this can lead them to be sensitive too to the emotional states of others.

In contrast are people who seem to be insensitive to the emotional states of others. These are individuals who appear to act in ways that suggest that they either are incapable of understanding the emotions of others or simply do not care. There is a scene in the movie *Fried Green Tomatoes* where a character who appears briefly steals one of the main character's parking spot and then makes a disparaging remark. This would seem to be the sort of person that does not recognize the emotional states of others and probably does not recognize their own emotions, including anger. People like this are often thought of as lacking empathy.

Yet the distinction between those that recognize their own emotions and those that are thought not to is not as clear cut as the person who gets their parking spot stolen and cries about it, and the other individual who does the "dastardly deed" and laughs with a sense of callous triumph. Sure, there are people like that in the world and many of us have interacted with them. Movies do have a tendency to exaggerate characters because they only have a limited amount of time to show you who someone is and they have to drive the point home.

But the reality is that even people who are thought to not recognize their emotions or to lack empathy may not be as heartless as we think they are. This discussion is being explored for a number of reasons, but mostly to introduce you to the idea that the various components of emotional intelligence and of empathy are related. Recognizing your emotions is important as an individual skill, but it should be used in tandem with having empathy, recognizing the emotions of others, self-regulation, and all the other skills that fall under the scope of emotional intelligence.

What we mean is that recognizing your emotions has the greatest value if you then use that as a starting point to also recognize the emotions of others. Recognizing your own emotions also is important to use a component of self-regulation, which as you recall refers to the ability to halt or redirect your own dysfunctional emotions. If you recognize your own emotions but then proceed to ignore the emotions of others, acting only with concern to how you think and how you feel, then you may simply be being narcissistic, which is a world away from exercising empathy.

We can explore this point further by going back to the example from *Fried Green Tomatoes*. It is clear that the character that becomes upset and understands why she is upset is recognizing her feelings. What is not clear is exactly what is going on with the other character. We assume that the other character is not recognizing their own feelings as they appear to be insensitive to the feelings of others. There is a tendency to lump people together into a giant cauldron of "people who do not care about feelings," when there are distinctions here that this sort of tactic blunts.

It is possible that the character that is behaving insensitively is recognizing her own feelings.

Recognizing your own feelings does not necessarily mean that you care deeply about the feelings of others. As we stated above, the significance of recognizing your feelings in the context of emotional intelligence and empathy is that you, in turn, use that to understand the feelings of others, show compassion, and have empathy. The character who is insensitive to the feelings of others may have felt emotions that guided her actions in contrast to what the viewer assumes.

This character — the driver who cuts off another driver, steals their parking spot, and then makes an ungenial remark – may have been angry because they were late or elated because they had found a parking spot and therefore did not have to worry about spending 10 minutes trying to find an appropriate one. These feelings of anger and elation are perfectly valid emotions. They are ones that individuals may recognize if they engage in the practice of attempting to recognize their emotions.

The problem here is that recognizing your own emotions does not necessarily mean that you behave in a way that indicates sympathy for the emotions of others. A narcissist is sensitive to their own emotions and desires, but that does not make them kind, caring, and compassionate people. A narcissist cares only about their own desires and motivations and acts with wanton disregard for the emotions and desires of others. A person who recognizes their own emotions but does not then assess, understand, and care about the emotions of others is exercising narcissistic behavior, which is harmful and insensitive to those individuals that find themselves in the narcissist's path.

This is an important distinction to make because some people focus on recognizing emotions and acting on them as a critical tool in emotional intelligence and empowerment, but all this endeavor really does is justify and encourage narcissism. Someone who decides that their sibling or child who has recently been in a car accident cannot come to stay with them temporarily because it is inconvenient may be recognizing their own emotions and acting on them, but they may be straying into a narcissistic territory.

It is important to explore this narcissistic dimension of recognizing emotions because this is a behavior pattern that is not only not empathy, but in direct opposition to empathy. By behaving narcissistically, we suck all of the empathy out of ourselves and others. We create a world where individuals are motivated by rage, personal gain, spite, and revenge. The power of empathy and emotional intelligence lies in being able to use emotions to form connections with people. If you care only about your own emotions and are insensitive to those of others, you are not forming connections, you are destroying them.

Recognizing Your Own Emotions as a Staging Ground

Recognizing your own emotions is the staging ground for then recognizing the emotions of others. This is why empathy and emotional intelligence do not consist of single emotional skills but several of them. This should lead people to understand that successful emotional intelligence involves tying several emotional steps together for the goal of interconnectivity. If all you are doing is recognizing your own emotions, then you are not understanding the emotions of others and you are ultimately not behaving with emotional intelligence.

Therefore, the next logical step after recognizing your own emotions is to then assess and understand the emotions of others. The driver who cuts off another driver may recognize that they are feeling anger because they are late, rage because someone else recently cut them off and they want revenge, or elation because they were not expecting to find a parking spot so quickly and they suddenly found one. They may recognize these emotions, but they then have to take a step back and assess the emotions of the other person(s) involved so as to behave with empathy and emotional intelligence.

The logical steps that a person in this situation should follow is to ask themselves: (1) are there any other people involved here I should be thinking about, (2) what are the emotions and desires of the others involved, (3) what is the significance of the emotions and desires of others relative to me and what I am about to do, and (4) how can I act in a way that shows that I am understanding the emotions of others and that I care about them.

Although some have argued that it is silly and insignificant to be constantly thinking about the emotions and desires of others, if you believe in emotional intelligence and its power, and you recognize that empathy is a skill that human beings should hone, then it is necessary for you to take steps to think about and try to understand the emotions of other people. If the character in the film had gone through these steps, she would have recognized that someone else had been waiting for that parking spot and that they may have been experiencing their own emotions of sadness, anger, and frustration. Once they have undertaken this sort of thought process, they would be reasonably expected to find another parking space out of sympathy or even empathy for the experiences of the other person involved.

Therefore, recognizing one's own emotions is a

starting point for behaving with empathy towards others. Indeed, recognizing individual emotions alone does not directly lead to sympathy, empathy, or emotional intelligence within ourselves. If men and women focus solely on recognizing their own emotions but do not care about the emotions of others, then they are actually behaving with narcissism which is the antithesis of the empathy that this book seeks to encourage.

It may seem a little frightening that narcissism and empathy can be so closely related, but life on Earth is filled with these sorts of dualities. Living successfully on this planet is about understanding the balance that is the natural state of life on Earth. As an animal species, we are meant to live in a measure of balance with members of our own species as well as members of other species. Thinking only of our own emotions and desires causes us to be out of balance and to then cause our environments to be out of balance. The simple act of a single person behaving narcissistically can lead to others also behaving the same way, which leads to a social group then becoming out of balance with the natural forces of nature.

Self-Regulation Should Work in Concert with Recognizing Your Emotions

An important component of recognizing your own emotions is regulating them, which is called self-regulation in emotional intelligence. Self-regulation means that you halt or alter your emotions based on the perception that your emotions may lead to dysfunction for yourself or for others. The reality is that emotions are a can of worms that can be both positive and negative. We can feel love that leads us to behave beneficently towards others, or we may feel anger that causes us to perhaps do things that are not so beneficent.

Even love can cause people to do things that are harmful or which should not be encouraged. Emotions are complicated, changing things and being in touch with them does not necessarily mean that we are behaving in a way that leads to a positive result. The reality is that sometimes it is necessary to regulate our emotions. Indeed, assessing whether or not you may need to regulate your emotions is an important part of being in touch with your emotions just as understanding the emotions of others is.

Regulating your own emotions will involve understanding what the results of acting on your emotions are. You can also think of this as the implications of your emotions. Your emotions may lead you to engage in an act that is beneficial to you, but harmful to someone else. Your emotions may also lead you to act impulsively, and acting impulsively frequently leads to actions that we later live to regret. By recognizing your own emotions in concert with self-regulation, you ensure that you are behaving in a way that takes into account how others are affected by our actions.

Behaving in this self-regulating manner prevents us from behaving narcissistically. By taking a moment to stop ourselves from acting based on emotion, we then can take that important step of assessing what the results of our actions are. Although it may seem time-consuming to constantly be going through these stages of doing first one mental/emotional task and then another, this will eventually become second nature. People who have empathy naturally or who are long practiced in having empathy immediately think about the implications that their actions have on others. The real power of recognizing your own emotions lies in then assessing what those emotions mean in the bigger picture of human interaction.

Activities That Can Improve Our Emotional State

Related to self-regulation is the idea that an individual may need to infuse calm into their personal space if they find that their emotions are making them heated or are causing them to behave in a way that is dysfunctional. There are many ways that an emotional state can be improved. Listening to calm, soothing music or thinking thoughts that make you happy or peaceful are methods to consider. Meditation and breathing exercise, in particular, are very powerful as they train the mind to appreciate peace and calm. They also cause you to understand the power and joy that comes from calmness and balance, causing you to naturally behave in ways that encourages calm.

Chapter 4

The Importance of Empathy

One of the hallmarks of human beings is our ability to form civilizations. Although we share this planet with other animal species, human beings alone are capable of forming the complex social structure that forms the basis of civilizations. Although it is not entirely clear why some groups of humans form civilizations and others do not, it is apparent that human beings are the only known species on planet Earth that possess the capability.

It is interesting to discuss empathy from the standpoint of civilization because it opens the door to another discussion: the discussion of what it is that makes human beings unique and ultimately whether we are truly unique at all. A quality of human beings closely related to empathy is altruism. Altruism is the ability to act selflessly. Altruistic people act toward the benefit of others even when these actions are detrimental to themselves. Biologists have actually discovered that human beings are not alone in behaving altruistically. As time goes on, more and more examples of altruism become evident in nature.

There are a bovine species in the savannas of Africa in which the members rescue a member of their pack that has been singled out by lions by crowding around their injured comrade, even though this means that they too may be attacked by lions and potentially skilled. Biologists have proposed that these acts of altruism in nature are all tied to the tendency for members within animal groups to be closely related, therefore sacrificing a member who is essentially a close relative confers direct benefit by preserving one's own DNA.

But interpretations of altruism in nature do not take full stock of the power of strange occurrences like altruism and empathy. A biologist can certainly argue that altruism may have evolved because members within a social group of animals tend to be closely related, but it would seem that preserving one's own genetic material would be more advantageous than preserving someone else's, even if they were closely related. And the ability of human beings to have empathy for people who they are not related to at all cannot be explained by this very empiric approach to animal behavior.

It is fairly well established in evolutionary biology that altruism results from natural selection. The belief being that animal behavior can always be linked to selection pressure. We have Charles Darwin to thank for the empirical manner in which science approaches incidences of animals behaving strangely, no matter how peculiar that behavior is. The idea of natural selection in animal behavior essentially hinges on the notion that behaviors that cause some individuals to survive better than others eventually become more frequent or common within the population.

In other words, taking altruism as our example, animals that exhibit altruism evolved to behave that way because those individuals that had this behavior survived better than those that did not behave altruistically. The animals that were altruistic are said to have enhanced *fitness* relative to the animals that were not altruistic. Fitness is the quality of surviving and propagating one's genetic material relative to the rest of the population.

This idea of fitness in animal behavior causes a conundrum but it leaves the door open to two ideas. One is that animal behavior can always be explained in terms of evolution. And the other idea (specific to this book) is that behaviors in human beings should also be explained by evolution. Even the most studied evolutionary biologist would probably say that just as altruism can be explained by natural selection, then so too should empathy be explained by this reasoning. But there is an aspect to this story that is not tackled by this purely pragmatic approach.

Evolution happens in the first place because diversity naturally exists within populations, and that includes genetic diversity. Non-human animals are easy subjects in behavioral biology and evolutionary biology because they tend to exhibit much less diversity than human beings. Individual members of animal species, including those that exhibit altruism, tend to be much more similar to one another than human beings are to one another, even in populations of human beings that exhibit relatively low diversity based solely on genes.

Perhaps you have already guessed the point that we are introducing here. Animal behavior cannot be purely explained by natural selection because of the unpredictable nature of genes (among other things). Even if science is able to explain the presence of altruism by resorting to natural selection theories stemming from Darwinism, this does not account for the reality that behaviors often linger even if they can be proven to be detrimental. Even if you choose to take a purely scientific approach to the subject, the idea that everything can be explained by natural selection can surely be shown to be simplistic. In evolution, genes are not easily isolated to the extent that one gene becomes the standard while another disappears completely. This is why in animals, we can generally observe qualities or behaviors that would appear to not be beneficial to the organism.

This subject can be applied to human beings, reticent

as we are to submerge the subject in evolutionary terms. It is interesting to ponder why humans developed empathy, the ability to experience the subjective emotions and experiences of others. The idea that human beings developed this ability by dent of being a highly socially interconnected species has been presented. But the idea of the evolution of this behavior, an evolution that resulted from pure concrete benefits that this behavior conferred has not been discussed.

Indeed, it can be argued that empathy has as many drawbacks as it has benefits. People who lack empathy often seem to live easier lives, lives free of the cares, depression, and physical stress that come from caring greatly about others. Some believe that people that lack empathy are more successful in certain occupations. They certainly appear to be good competitors, and many famous leaders throughout history we could probably agree lacked empathy, or at least suppressed it extremely well.

Therefore the issue then becomes why human beings feel empathy when one can argue that those without empathy would seem to have an evolutionary advantage over those that do show this capability. The answer is something that we touched on, but which might not be apparent because issues of emotion often are difficult for the mind to grasp in concrete ways. There are two possibilities here. One is that empathy actually does confer a fitness advantage, which has caused it to be preserved as a human characteristic for thousands of years. The other possibility is that empathy is so intrinsic to being a higher functioning animal that it cannot be bred out of us even by evolution.

Think about it this way. We can say that trait A confers advantages to a human population so it should, therefore, become present in all individuals over a long period of time. We can also say that trait B confers disadvantages to human beings so it should eventually disappear over time. But if trait B is the requirement for water then it is not possible that this requirement will ever be bred out of a population because it is necessary for the population to survive.

Feeling empathy as part of forming a connection with

other human beings may be the water that we drink to sustain us. Those that never feel empathy may live long lives, but they never live the full experience of being human. Those who are empathic not only are able to have better relationships with others, but they also are sensitive to the world around them in ways that others are not. Individuals who seem to lack empathy may appear to have advantages over empathic individuals because life is easier for them in some ways as they do not have to feel things, but any advantage they may have is nullified by the disadvantage of missing out on high emotional intelligence and the experiences that come along with it.

The Skills of Empathy

Empathy, therefore, becomes something important and potentially essential to human beings. This is why empathy has persisted in our species in spite of the advantages that may come from being a Genghis Khan or a Tamerlane. Somehow, empathy is so significant to human beings that nature cannot take it away from us even if it may want to. So the matter then becomes how people can become more empathetic.

Studies have shown that human beings can become more empathetic by talking about empathy. Although this has specifically been shown to be true for the workplace, it is also true of anyone attempting to infuse more empathy into their lives. Talking about empathy permits our thinking to change, making empathy into a pattern that becomes normal for us. Neural patterns develop in the brain through repetition, so talking about empathy and subsequently having empathy is the perfect jumping off point for changing the role that empathy has in our lives.

Empathy can be broken down into the realms of (1) empathic accuracy, (2) empathic compassion, and (3) empathic interactions. As can be gleamed from these descriptive terms, empathy, even when taken on as a subject distinct from emotional intelligence, does seem to overlap with emotional intelligence in terms of how it is defined.

Not unlike the step of accurately assessing and

interpreting the emotional cues from others that is part of emotional intelligence, empathic accuracy involves the accurate perception that comes from interacting with others and which leads to having empathy. By accurately assessing the emotions and experiences of others, we are able to have empathy for them. If one were to make an inaccurate assessment – for example detecting anger when there is really sadness – then your own reaction will be inaccurate because it is based on an inaccurate initial perception. And from a holistic standpoint, the connection becomes jilted because the emotions of both parties do not accurately correspond to one another.

Empathic compassion is the sympathetic component of empathy. Like many terms in emotional intelligence, empathic compassion is not fully distinct from the compassion that defines sympathy, just as empathy is not fully distinct from emotional intelligence. This lack of clear distinction in terms is part of what confuses people about the subject, but it is also a way emotional intelligence should be approached differently than cognitive ability or other concepts in psychology that were designed to be clearly demarcated and measured.

Essential to empathic compassion is feeling the tolerance and goodwill relationship that one also feels when one feels sympathy for another. In the case of empathy, this type of compassion is the beginning to forming the deeper connection that comes with sharing the feelings of the other person. Where sympathy stops, empathy is just beginning.

Empathic interactions are the bonds that result in feeling another person's subjective experiences. Once you have accurately understood where the other person is coming from, and once you have felt compassion for the other person as a result of that basic understanding, then you are able to have an empathic interaction. This interaction is important because this is the conclusion that is meant to result from the two other components of empathy. Just as people can recognize their own feelings without necessarily recognizing another person's feelings, so too can we feel sympathy without necessarily sharing in another person's experiences.

Although men and women who have never felt true empathy may find it difficult to understand how one person can share another person's subjective experiences, research has suggested that true empathy can be learned. There are steps that one can follow to help one become better with empathy. Here is a simple breakdown that some may find useful.

- Talk about empathy
- Practice empathy
- Focus on forming an accurate assessment of other's emotions and experiences during interactions
- Focus on feeling compassion for others during interactions
- Focus on having interactions that are based on accurate assessments and compassion

Chapter 5

Building Solid Relationships

Emotions are a tricky subject because it involves matters in which people tend to use terminology without necessarily understanding what the terminology means. Frequently, terminology pertaining to emotion is used incorrectly, or it is used in such a way that it has been stripped of its real meaning. We may say that certain people are emotional, but it is not clear what that means. Even the person who uses the term emotional might be using it differently than how the person hearing it interprets it. Because emotional intelligence involves interactions, it is easy for emotional intelligence to be stymied because people use improper terminology or allow themselves to be misled by terms that have acquired a negative connotation.

Typically, when someone is described as emotional,

this is intended to be taken in a negative light. People who are emotional are often regarded as impulsive, difficult to talk to, difficult to work with, unscientific, irrational, loud, or resistant to being spoken to. But this characterization is based on assumptions about people that are emotional. Indeed, labeling someone as emotional is a simple and almost devious way to neutralize and invalidate someone by immediately labeling them as something which they may or may not be.

Words have power and in using words incorrectly and communicating them to people, we allow those words to become a part of that person because now others will come to associate that person with those words that we have chosen to label them with. In labeling someone emotional, we have now doomed them to being interpreted in a specific light by others that they will be interacting with. This prevents them from being able to build social relationships and sustain them in a way that is healthy and beneficial for both.

Building social relationships is the end goal of

emotional intelligence and highly emotionally intelligent people have been shown to have better social relationships with others. This leads to highly emotionally intelligent people being more successful in objective measures of success. "Emotional" people are thought to be better at relationships, but this is because "emotional" people are considered to think about emotions more than others do.

This perception has to do with the idea that thinking about emotions too much is something negative. These dysfunctional perceptions have led to some people eschewing in any and all emotion, while others have taken the opposite side and have become advocates for emotion and emotional thinking. But this is really a downward spiral that results from terminology not being used appropriately in the case of emotion. Showing compassion for someone is a sign that you feel emotion. All religions are infused with emotional feeling and people become better friends, better family members, and better lovers because they care.

Emotion is the basis for meaningful social

relationships. Having emotions does not mean that you are bogged down by them, which is how some characterize the term. By rejecting emotion or mischaracterizing emotion, we create a society where people either have distorted emotions because they do not understand them correctly or they feel no emotion at all because they have been taught to be wary of emotion based on misconceptions about emotion.

An easy way to think about emotion as the basis for building relationships is by thinking about how we actually relate to one another. When you engage in an act that is beneficial to someone other than yourself, you are showing emotion. Perhaps it is part of your spiritual or religious belief to engage in acts that show charity or kindness towards others. Perhaps you have donated clothes to a charitable organization or have provided assistance at a soup kitchen. These are all ways that you show care and concern for others.

Caring, concern, worry — these are all feelings that fall along the spectrum with sadness, anger, guilt, disappointment, hope, and all the other feelings that are part of being human. These are things that people should not run from but should embrace as they are essential to partaking in social relationships with others.

In this chapter, the data showing the relationship benefits of emotional intelligence will not be explored as this point has been belabored in other chapters. Suffice it to say that research suggests that highly emotionally intelligent people have better relationships and more successful group interactions than people who do not demonstrate emotional intelligence. Of course, these benefits stem from all aspects of emotional intelligence. People that have empathy, have better self-regulation skills or demonstrate compassion will generally be liked and valued by their peers compared to people who are not.

One of the goals of this chapter is not to approach the issue of emotion from the standpoint of two camps: those in favor of emotional thinking and those against it. This dichotomy approaches the subject from a distorted standpoint as it does not accept that feeling emotions are a normal part of being human. Indeed, lacking emotion or demonstrating emotion in an irregular way is a criterion for some psychiatric conditions in the Diagnostic and Statistical Manual. The goal of this book is not therefore to lead you to see this subject from the standpoint of being an "emotional person" or an "unemotional (or rational) person." We all feel emotions and we need to claim them.

By understanding how having emotions ties into the many aspects of emotional intelligence, we are able to approach the subject in a healthy way. Some of the stigma that comes from so-called emotional people is that people that have been labeled as emotional may not engage in the associated steps of understanding other people's emotions, self-regulation, and empathy. This was touched on in the discussion of narcissism, but those who embrace their emotions in a healthy way also embrace the emotions of others and know how to regulate their emotions if they begin to get in the way of social interactions.

Social relationships, therefore, require that all the

components of emotional intelligence be used effectively. Indeed, the topic of healthy social relationships helps tie together the power of emotional intelligence as a tool as it does not focus merely on one area. In order to build and maintain social relationships, an individual must:

- Demonstrate compassion and tolerance for others
- Have empathy
- Assess one's emotions and the emotions of others
- Understand the emotions of others
- Make an effort to relate to others
- Regulate one's own emotions

Social relationships are complex, whether they are romantic in nature, friendships, or employer-employee relationships. By tying together all aspects of emotional intelligence, men and women can create and maintain important relationships. This is not just true of individuals in the workplace. Research has shown clearly that going through the different intelligences that comprise emotional intelligence is important for adults in their personal relationships and children in the school setting.

Chapter 6

Non-Verbal Communication

Non-verbal communication is essential to social interactions in humans. Although human beings do have the capability of producing speech, the cues that we send that do not involve words are just as important in conveying our feelings, desires, and intentions as the words that we say. Non-verbal communication is almost a form of mind-reading, which can be both positive and negative. By communicating without words, sometimes we can express how we feel more accurately and more deeply. As a song from the 90s goes: "Words are meaningless, especially sentences." It is not always easy to describe what we are feeling with words.

Non-verbal communication is sometimes overlooked because everyone does it so it is easy to take it for granted. Overlooked or not, non-verbal communication is important as it allows to be cued in to what we are feeling or thinking. Recall that empathy and emotional intelligence, in general, requires that the other person be able to accurately gauge our emotions and experiences. This means that non-verbal communication comprises a set of non-verbal cues that others will use to be able to accurately gauge what we feel.

This is important because it means that we must be keyed in not only to the non-verbal cues of others but to our own cues that we are sending. This is distinct from the self-regulation that is part and parcel of emotional intelligence, but there are some similarities. Sometimes it may be important to curtail our negative cues or cues that may push people away even if they reflect how we feel. Although this may seem to some like dishonesty, it is really just a recognition that interactions with others are important and that sometimes we have to coordinate and control our own cues so as to be able to interact with others. The assumption here is that others will be engaging in a similar dance of regulation of non-verbal cues, and this is all a part of normal human interaction.

The question then becomes what the non-verbal cues are that others are responding to. There are many gestures, movements, postures, and other things that we do as people to indicate what we are feeling internally. Some of these are gestures that naturally crop up as a result of our internal state, like the furrowed brow that indicates worry, while others are acquired postures that we pick up sometimes without knowing, like placing your hands on your hips when you are irritated, angry, or in a hurry.

No matter where our gestures originate, it is important to be conscious of them so that we can think about how our gestures may be interpreted by others. Although the argument can be made that we should not alter these non-verbal cues as they accurately reflect how we feel, sometimes it is necessary to control our own emotion (or indications of our emotion) as part of showing sympathy or having empathy for others.

Being conscious of our non-verbal cues, therefore, becomes an essential part of the social interactions that we have with others. People who frequently show non-verbal cues that indicate negative or frustrated emotions will likely be perceived more negatively by people than those whose gestures are more positive. Although everyone goes through trying times and everyone naturally feels anger, sadness, frustration, tiredness, and the like, paying attention to our social cues can help us get along better with others and have more fruitful outcomes from our interactions.

Examples abound of the sort of cues that we send that indicate how we are feeling. People often use our cues as a more accurate indication of what we feel than our words. Examples include saying how excited you are to be invited to the wedding of the person you are talking to, but then yawning when he or she describes the details. Perhaps you are a manager and you tell a subordinate that you are happy to hear their concerns about the job, but you are grimacing the entire time. It can be useful to think about how our non-verbal cues may contradict our words. When this happens, the listener may become confused, irritated, or perceive us as someone who does not have sympathy for themselves.

Although most people will be familiar with the sorts of non-verbal cues that indicate our internal emotional state, it may be helpful to some people to review them here. Some of these non-verbal cues include:

- Body position
- Facial expression
- Hand position
- Yawning
- Laughter
- Hands on hips
- Speed of speech
- Tapping of the foot
- Vocal Tone
- Looking away or not making eye contact

These are all ways that we show the person that we are interacting with that we are or are not interested in speaking with them. Highly emotionally intelligent people are conscious of these sorts of gestures when they interact with others. Resilient people also are conscious of these gestures because they understand how important in life successful interactions are.

Indeed, resilient people know that life can take a turn for the worse at any moment and you may need a helping hand to help pull you back up. By focusing on the power of non-verbal cues in social interactions, you can become more resilient both by maintaining better relationships and by infusing more positivity into your body and your life.

By paying attention to the cues listed above, you can effectively show sympathy, have empathy, and set yourself on the path towards becoming a highly emotionally intelligent individual.

Chapter 7

Thirty Facts to Help You Be More Emotionally Intelligent

Highly emotionally intelligent individuals are sensitive to the emotions and desires of the people around them. The modern psychological approach to emotional intelligence and attempts to measure this capability reflect the realities of intelligence quotients and other tests, but it does draw some indirect inspiration from older perceptions of human capabilities. Eastern religions had much to say about the place of human beings in the world and the interconnectivity of all living things. In spite of all the tests and measures, the very idea of emotional intelligence harkens back to perceptions about innate abilities that human beings have to form connections with one another.

Empathy, in particular, emphasizes the unsaid aspects

of human connection and human interaction. One person can feel another's pain or experience other emotions of theirs with no cues at all. This suggests that there are aspects of emotional intelligence that will never be fully quantified by tests. Tests can attempt to capture the results or benefits of emotional intelligence, but what emotional intelligence really is and where it comes from will always be somewhat of a mystery.

This mystery can be demystified by consolidating information about emotional intelligence in an easily digestible way. This is an important endeavor to undertake on this subject because the information is so heterogeneous as to represent a daunting task to the average person who works a 9 to 5 and does not necessarily have the time to read three hardcover books and ten journal articles just to learn the basics. You have an idea of what emotional intelligence is, you have an idea of how it can benefit you, and you have an idea of how you can use it practically. Now it is time for you to synthesize all of this information into facts that put the pieces of this wide canvas into one complete whole.

Fact 1: Empathy involves feeling compassion for others while also relating to the experiences and emotions of others.

Empathy is a quality that some are born with and that others develop over time. Some become empathic by assessing their own emotional states and recognizing that they have problems relating to other people. One this recognition is made, we can learn to change the way we relate to others and interact with them. Empathy is important because it represents a quality that cannot fully be quantified or even understood by science.

But what is empathy? Sympathy is the act of showing tolerance and feeling compassion for others. Empathy takes this one step further by adding to this the ability to experience the subjective emotional state of others. By feeling another's joy, another's pain, another's sadness, we are relating to them in a way that is among the deepest connections that we can have with another person. This empathy is the basis for the altruism that human beings are capable of, a capability that takes us beyond the realm of mere animals and into the world of becoming human.

Fact 2: Empathy is an important component of emotional intelligence, one of several skills that fall under the emotional intelligence umbrella.

Even people who are familiar with emotional intelligence are not always clear on where exactly empathy falls in the big picture. Empathy involves both skills that can be utilized by actively thinking, but it also involves feeling another person's emotion, which makes it distinct from other components typically associated with emotional intelligence. Different schools of thought on emotional intelligence approach the subject from alternative angles, but it can be said that empathy is one of several abilities that fall under the guise of emotional intelligence.

These abilities utilized together allow individuals to not only be perceptive of the emotions and desires of others, but to also behave in a way that demonstrates understanding. When the empathy component comes in, there is also the unspoken connection that comes from the subjective experience of emotion. This makes emotional intelligence something powerful, but it also makes it something difficult to quantify or fully understand.

Fact 3: Emotional intelligence has been studied for more than 50 years and the work continues.

Some readers may have been only marginally familiar with emotional intelligence when they picked up this book and that is because it is a relatively new concept. Emotional intelligence as a term was coined in the mid-60s and it was later made popular by a best-selling book written by psychologist Daniel Goleman. This book presented the belief that emotional intelligence might be more important than IQ, a term that many Americans would have been familiar with because of controversy surrounding disparities in IQ results.

But the studies around emotional intelligence have long been fraught with difficulties. There is not a consensus on what emotional intelligence is, and many people within the psychological community dispute its relevance. In spite of the naysayers, emotional intelligence continues to be a hot topic in part because of its ties to empathy, which is a capability that many people feel. Because people understand the importance of empathy, they often are more amenable to appreciating the relevance of emotional intelligence.

Fact 4: Studies suggest that empathy is essential to effective leadership.

Many studies have been conducted about the practical relevance of emotional intelligence. In part, this reflects the need to convince people that this skill set is real and important, but it also is an attempt to help everyday people infuse emotional intelligence into their lives. Much of the studies around emotional intelligence hone in on workplace dynamics, and it has been found that in this arena, emotional intelligence is particularly important.

Emotional intelligence (specifically, empathy) has been shown to be an essential part of effective leadership. Leaders that demonstrate empathy are rated higher by their employees and are generally more successful in their leadership pursuits. Empathy is so critical in fact that many organizations have organized training and commissioned manuals to teach their leadership how to be emotionally intelligent.

Fact 5: There are three major models of emotional intelligence.

Emotional intelligence has been defined by three models that seek to take it away from the realm of the amorphous and make it into a distinct set of capabilities that can be measured and tested in psychology. The three models of emotional intelligence are the ability model, the trait model, and the mixed model. There are some differences between the models, but they all make a list of specific skills that they consider to fall under the purview of emotional intelligence. They also address the issue of whether emotional intelligence is intelligence or if it is something else.

Although some psychologists focus on one particular model that they believe and that they test (as each model has its own tests and measures), many choose to use these models to create a gestalt that helps them understand all aspects of emotional intelligence.

Synthesizing these models, we can say that emotional intelligence comprises a set of different capabilities that can be measured just as one would measure intelligence quotient.

Fact 6: Some psychologists have suggested that emotional intelligence is a type of intelligence not unlike cognitive reasoning.

One of the most controversial subjects within EI is the idea of whether it is intelligence. Some have suggested that emotional intelligence should actually be considered a skill that is based on cognitive ability, but this approach fails to take stock of empathy and self-regulation, abilities that have little or nothing to do with traditional cognition.

Part of the reason why some see emotional intelligence as being like cognitive ability (or traditional intelligence) can be traced to a desire to put this more holistic skill on par with abilities that have traditionally been measured by tests. But this approach also falls into the trap of a tit for tat argument with one side arguing over the relative merits of their type of intelligence over the other. By accepting emotional intelligence as a set of skills that are important and can be measured, EI can be made practical and the relevance of whether or not it is intelligence can become, well, irrelevant.

Fact 7: Emotional intelligence is a skill that can be learned.

One of the most powerful aspects of EI is that it can be learned. Because emotional intelligence can be learned, executives or other members of higher leadership can train their leaders and deputies to have emotional intelligence. Studies have shown that emotional intelligence is correlated with better leadership, happier employees, and improved outcomes in the workplace.

Fact 8: Emotional intelligence is relevant to all aspects of a person's life.

The workplace is just one setting where emotional intelligence can be powerful. Studies have suggested that emotional intelligence leads to better intimate relationships and better relationships with family. People who are emotionally intelligent get along better with others, which makes them happier and more successful in whatever endeavor they pursue.

Because emotional intelligence draws on the basic reality of human interconnectivity, any setting in which humans interact with other humans will benefit from EI. By accurately assessing the emotional states of others and responding in appropriate ways, we are able to foment important connections that lead to benefits for the person utilizing this capability.

Fact 9: Some psychologists measure emotional intelligence using self-report, which has caused some controversy in the field because of false reporting.

There are many aspects of emotional intelligence that have sparked debates in the social science community. Although many people recognize the importance of empathy, some of the technical aspects of emotional intelligence, especially the tests that purport to measure emotional intelligence capability, have become a source of detractors of this concept.

Not all emotional intelligence measures are the same,

but many tests of emotional intelligence (not to mention measures that seek to gauge the importance of EI) involve self-reporting. The person completing the assessment rates their own emotional intelligence skills and often makes an assessment of how important they think their own skills are. Although there is some clear utility to this type of measure, it is not difficult to understand why some would be skeptical of this approach. Ratings of one's one capabilities can easily lead to false reports.

Fact 10: Some psychologists warn that emotional intelligence can be used to manipulate, but others posit that manipulation or persuasion can be used to benefit others.

The manipulation aspect of EI is an important subject to know about because it is something that people sometimes bring up. The idea here is that highly emotionally intelligent people, that is, those who are very keyed in to the emotional states of others, can use that information to their own benefit. They can share information they have gathered with others supposedly to harm the person or force them to do something that they perhaps do not wish to do.

But an important aspect of manipulation is persuasion. Even if we say that emotional intelligence can be used to manipulate, that position does not necessarily mean that emotional intelligence is itself a malign to. Persuasion can and has been used to help people by guiding them in a positive direction. EI used this way is of benefit and so this charge of manipulation is unjust.

Fact 11: Effective leaders need to be able to communicate not only with their employees but with people from other companies and from other cultures. This renders emotional intelligence a critical skill to have.

Much of recent research on EI has focused on the workplace. It has been consistently found that leaders that demonstrate empathy are perceived more positively by their employees and are typically more successful in their leadership roles. There are a number of reasons why empathy is important in effective leaders. As it stands, most employees are not robots all pumped out of an assembly line. This means that a leader has to deal with employees that are different from one another and different from the manager.

By demonstrating emotional intelligence, a leader is able to show that they empathize with others regardless of their background. Skills like repeating what someone says to show that you have heard and understand are simple ways to infuse EI into an interaction. Although empathy is sometimes more difficult to train because it requires that one feels another's emotions, if a leader is able to truly have empathy, then the possibilities of his leadership role are endless.

Fact 12: Important components of emotional intelligence include recognizing your own emotions, accurately assessing the internal state of others, and understanding where others are coming from.

Emotional intelligence can be defined differently based on which model of EI you choose to identify with, but it can be summarized as the ability to assess your own feelings, assess accurately the emotional state of others, understanding where others are coming from in a particular moment in time, and showing tolerance and compassion. In this way, emotional intelligence integrates empathy, sympathy, and other skills that allow us to connect better with others.

Fact 13: An important component of emotional intelligence is self-regulation. Self-regulation is also a critical part of many psychological coping mechanisms.

Self-regulation is a very important part of emotional intelligence and one that sometimes gets overlooked. Self-regulation involves halting or altering your own thoughts or emotions because they may be dysfunctional. What this means on a practical basis is that sometimes you may find yourself reacting to others based on their gestures, words, or something else about the person. Although some may argue that it is normal for human beings to form reactions to things, negative reactions can be perceived by others and can hurt their feelings.

By being conscious of our own thoughts and

regulating them, we are able to have more successful interactions with others by removing any negativity that can adversely affect the interaction. Although self-regulation is not mentioned in all three models of emotional intelligence, a holistic definition that synthesizes the components of all three should take stock of this, one of the more critical components of EI.

Fact 14: Emotional intelligence is key to successful relationships and is part of our patrimony as primates.

Emotional intelligence is not merely something that popped out of nowhere in the last 50 years. EI is a term that seeks to define a set of skills that have allowed humans to have successful interactions since essentially the beginning of the species. Emotional intelligence allowed humans to correctly assess what others were thinking and feeling in order to avert danger, but also to form relationships that were mutually beneficial to both parties.

If human beings had not developed emotional intelligence skills, they would not have been able to form large, complex societies because they would not have been able to interact with one another effectively. EI allows us to understand others in such a way that we can have these effective interactions. If we are unable to achieve this understanding, then interactions become stilted, confusing, and meaningless. This is of no benefit to us as individuals or as a species.

Fact 15: Empathy and other emotional skills are more important now than ever because of the increasing societal conflict caused by multiple factors.

Because of social forces that have caused us to become disconnected from one another in various ways, emotional intelligence is more important now than it has ever been before. Most men and women today do not live in communities where they have sustained interactions with people in the community so they are not always able to gauge the emotions and intentions of others based solely on familiarity. Through emotional intelligence skills, we can accurately assess the emotions of people that we may only be meeting in passing. This prevents us from being keyed up to anger or other negativity because of inaccurate assumptions.

Fact 16: An essential component of emotional intelligence is non-verbal communication, which involves how we communicate our internal state to others.

Non-verbal communication is one of those things that everyone knows is important, but which often gets overlooked. Non-verbal communication is important for a number of reasons, not least of which is that it allows us to gauge what others are thinking or feeling. Non-verbal communication also allows others to be keyed in to how we are thinking and feeling. Although non-verbal communication often gets left out of the emotional intelligence discussion, it is essential to be conscious of it and to practice it because this aspect of EI often is what causes us to have fruitless interaction with others.

Aspects of ourselves like our facial expression, body position, hand position, or other things that we do to indicate how we feel let others know these feelings even if they are in contradiction to our words. You can say that you care what the other is saying and that you are listening, but if your body language indicates otherwise or you are yawning, then you have sent a message that perhaps you do not care or your thoughts and concerns lie elsewhere.

Fact 17: Ways that we communicate non-verbally include gestures, speech speed, facial expressions, and vocal tone.

The list of non-verbal communication cues is very long. Fortunately, most people reading this have a general idea of the sorts of things people do to demonstrate an interest in the conversation or lack thereof. Common non-verbal cues that we sent to indicate how we are feeling include facial expression, vocal tone, speech speed, and gestures. By being conscious of these aspects of our communication, we can show the other person that we consider their feeling important enough to devote time to them and that we, in general, care about what is being said to us. These are all ways to demonstrate sympathy and put emotional intelligence to good and powerful use.

Fact 18: Showing empathy is not the same as having empathy.

Empathy is one of those things that people believe they understand but then have difficulty defining. Empathy is the ability to relate to and feel the emotions of others. This makes it distinct from sympathy, which hinges on compassion, tolerance, and understanding. But showing empathy is not the same as having empathy. We show empathy through our words and through our gestures. But actually feeling empathy is something only we know.

The reason why having empathy is important is because it dictates how we interact with people. If you do not feel empathy for others, then you are merely pretending to care about what they are saying. If you actually feel empathy, then you not only are making your life easier by not having to pretend to care, but you may actually help someone who may be looking for a positive interaction from you or for support.

Fact 19: Although empathy is correlated with job performance in many different countries around

the world, empathy appears to be more important in some cultures than in others.

All humans can feel empathy. Empathy is one of those constants in human beings that exist across borders. But studies have suggested that empathy may be more significant in some places than in others, at least as far as leadership and job performance goes. Studies have shown that in countries in which there is a high relative distance between management and employees, empathy is more important. That is, empathy is less important where the hierarchy between manager and managed is less pronounced.

There have been theories attempting to expound on this finding, but most agree that in cultures where the little people are really little (bear with us here), the need for empathy is greater because there is a power dynamic that tends to make the interaction between the manager and the managed more significant. If your manager is dressed the same as you are, makes the same money as you do, does not directly supervise you, or could not fire you even if he or she wanted, then it may be less important that they show empathy than in the case where your manager has your life in his or her hands.

Fact 20: An important component of empathy is active listening.

One can write an entire book on empathy and let's face it, some people have. The purpose of this book is not to harp on empathy, but this quality is such an important one to develop that it is hard not to keep bringing it up. An important way of showing others that you empathize with them is by demonstrating active listening. Active listening includes most of the common things that people think of like nodding your head and maintaining eye contact, but it also includes summarizing what the other person has said, using your words to show that you have understood what they have said, and saying things that demonstrate both understanding and sympathy. By doing all of these, you can not only put empathy to good use but teach yourself how to be more empathetic through this constant usage.

Fact 21: Others are not able to read our minds so

our words are important indicators of how we think and feel.

Just as we use the things that others say to us to gauge what others are thinking and feeling, so too do they use our words to gauge our own thoughts, desires, feelings, and intentions. Most of us do not have the ability to read minds so we must use the cues that they give us to learn what their feelings are. The words that we say show sympathy, which is a way for us to show that we are not only listening actively but that we care. Even the simple step of summarizing what another has said to us can show that we care.

Fact 22: Training, developmental initiatives, and coaching are all ways in which empathy can be learned.

There are men and women called empaths who seem able to feel the subjective pains, worries, love, and sadness of others almost on an instant. These individuals have these abilities without ever having to be taught them. Most of us are not empaths, which means that though we may have some skills in the empathy department, many of us would benefit from putting some time and effort into improving our empathy skillset.

Empathy can be learned. In fact, empathy can be learned well enough that organizations have devoted millions of dollars to empathy trainings and training manuals to help their employees become more empathetic. This is especially important when it comes to those in leadership roles, as studies have shown that lack of empathy can lead to the perception of poor management among staff and disaffection.

Fact 23: Studies suggest that half of all managers are rated poorly by their employees and can benefit from emotional intelligence training.

The previous discussion leads us right in (conveniently) to our next discussion on management training. Research suggests that 50% of managers are rated poorly by employees within organizations. This has been attributed to a failure of managers to show empathy, which causes employees to feel that their lives, concerns, and feelings are not valid. The last thing a manager wants to do is invalidate an employee. When all is said and done, as a manager, you need the employees more than they need you in many cases. By showing your staff that you care, you are able to create a staff that is loyal to you and willing to work hard for you. This is why emotional intelligence training is so important for organizations.

Fact 24: Lower emotional intelligence has been linked with being involved in incidents of bullying.

Recent studies have shown an interesting link between emotional intelligence and bullying. Studies suggest that individuals involved in bullying have been found to score low on emotional intelligence testing. What may be interesting to some is the finding that this includes all of the individuals involved in the bullying dynamic, including both the bully and the person being bullied. Although it may be clear why a bully would score low on emotional intelligence tests, it is not entirely clear why this is also true of the bullied individual.

Bullies often do not feel empathy for others, which

would explain their low scores on emotional intelligence tests. Bullied individuals, on the other hand, may be isolated from the group or have few meaningful social interactions with others. This makes them targets for bullies. Although the bullied person is not responsible for the bullying, the bully is able to pick up on the lack of what we might think of as emotional intelligence in the prospective bully, even if we are saying that the bully herself or himself has low emotional intelligence. These are murky waters as you can see, and hopefully, further research can clarify the subject somewhat.

Fact 25: Emotional intelligence has been shown to lead to more successful social interactions in children.

Some studies have focused on the relative importance of emotional intelligence in children. These studies have shown that children who are perceived as having higher emotional intelligence have more successful interactions with other children. These highly emotionally intelligent children have more friends, are liked by their peers, and in general are perceived more positively in group dynamics in the school setting.

Fact 26: High emotional intelligence does not mean conformity.

One controversy surrounding the subject of emotional intelligence has to do with conformity. It has been argued that all emotional intelligence does is enforce conformity, which does seem to be supported by at least some of the research conducted on the subject. Men and women who score high in emotional intelligence are rated more positively by their peers, have more successful personal relationships and interactions with others, and are generally more successful in their endeavors than those who are believed to be less emotionally intelligent.

The issue is the idea that people perceive others who show signs of understanding and relating to others, that is, sharing their feelings and belief on some level, are rated more positively by others. Someone who shows signs of not relating to us or who do not go out of their way to show sympathy would be less emotionally intelligent and would score more poorly in measures. There is, therefore, an element of sameness here, but hopefully, further research can clarify the subject a bit.

Fact 27: Emotional intelligence can be used to manipulate with negative intent, but that does not mean it should be used to that effect.

Correctly assessing the feelings of others can put you in a position of power over there. By being keyed in to the feelings of others, you can use this knowledge, for it is a form of knowledge for gain. This has been posited as a downside to pushing for emotional intelligence training or advocating for emotional intelligence in general. With that said, emotional intelligence should be used to have positive interactions with others. If your intentions are to do harm to others through interaction with them, then you have not really understood what empathy is and you might benefit from a little more reading on the subject.

Fact 28: Studies suggest that the first step that organizations can make towards improved emotional intelligence among their staff is to talk about empathy.

Organizations have a vested interest in encouraging empathy among their staff. This can include trainings, manuals, or group sessions that are centered around the subject of empathy. But the best first step that an organization can do to foster an environment where emotional intelligence is valued is to talk about empathy. Upper-level management can discuss empathy with their managers with the goal of guiding them on the way to being more empathetic to their staff.

Talking about empathy can include asking managers if they know what empathy is and how to use it. This does not have to take the form of training. It can be an informal discussion on the subject with the goal of putting a little seed in the managers' head that will germinate until it sprouts fruit. An effective approach may also include demonstrating to management the studies that have shown how empathy can lead to more effective teams. This is the start of a foray into empathy that will provide benefit to the organization, the manager, and the staff under the manager's care. The staff will appreciate the results that began with nothing more than a simple, straightforward discussion of the subject.

Fact 29: Human beings may not be alone in being able to have empathy.

Much has been written on the subject of animal nature in contrast to human nature. Indeed, in some religions, it is assumed that human beings have both animal nature and human nature and that the animal side of our selves may actually be stronger than the human side. These discourses are not meant to discourage humans, or to cause them to revert to what is often seen as brutal, animal characteristics. The idea in the past has been to point out that humans are often frustrating to deal with because we do have this animal nature that always seems to rear its head.

Closer examinations of other animals suggest that we may not be alone in having "human nature." If we construe human nature to consist of the concepts of empathy and altruism, then it becomes a distinct possibility that we are not alone in being constituted this way. Science abounds with examples of altruism in many animal species, a subject that has long baffled the community, which was taught to view animal behavior from the standpoint of natural selection and evolution.

Although science has successfully explained altruism by positing that members of a group in a particular animal species will risk their lives for other members that are closely related to them, this explanation still does not seem to fully grasp the ways that other animal species seem to live in connection with other members of their own species and with species entirely distinct from their own. Indeed, there are species that seem to be much better with this interconnectivity idea than we are. We may never be able to prove that animals can have empathy, but it is an interesting subject to ponder.

Fact 30: Recognizing our own emotions without understanding the emotions of others can cause

us to behave narcissistically.

Emotional intelligence is often thought of as a set of capabilities, but this does not mean that we should pick and choose which components of emotional intelligence we would like to use. Recognizing our emotions is an important component of emotional intelligence, but it needs to be used in tandem with other aspects of EI like assessing the emotions of others, making an attempt to understand these emotions, self-regulating our emotions, and showing sympathy for others.

Self-regulation is one of the EI skills that work most closely with recognizing our emotions because it allows us to halt or change those emotions that may cause us to behave with dysfunction. If we are conscious only of our own emotions and desires, and if we act solely based on these, then we are wandering into the shark-infested waters of the narcissist. Though some may not appreciate why narcissism is problematic, behaving in this fashion creates an environment where everyone is acting based solely on their own interests and desires, without the consideration for others feelings, or without an appreciation for how we are all interconnected. By recognizing our own emotions as a first step to recognizing the emotions of others, we are able to create more fulfilling connections with other people.

Frequently Asked Questions

1. What is emotional intelligence?

Emotional intelligence is the capability to accurately assess and understand another's emotional state, understand your own emotional state, and to feel compassion and tolerance towards others. This is a basic definition of emotional intelligence. There are different models of this concept that approach the idea differently. One model adds self-regulation to the capabilities of emotional intelligence, with self-regulation being the ability to halt your own emotional reaction to another person. Emotional intelligence has been demonstrated to be an important leadership quality. Some researchers have also suggested that it is not merely a capability (or range of capabilities), but a form of intelligence.

2. Is there a difference between emotional intelligence and empathy?

Like everything else in the emotional intelligence world, clearly distinguished emotional intelligence from empathy is a task that has not led to a general consensus. An important model of emotional intelligence sees emotional intelligence as a range of capabilities of which empathy is just one. This makes sense if we consider that there are parts of emotional intelligence that fall outside the realm of traditional empathy, such as self-regulation and demonstrating that you understand (rather than merely sharing an emotion).

3. Is empathy the same as sympathy?

People often confuse sympathy and empathy, and it is not hard to see why. Sympathy involves showing compassion and tolerance towards others. Although empathy also involves demonstrating these qualities, an intrinsic component of empathy is feeling or experiencing another's emotions or experiences. Demonstrating that you have compassion is not exactly the same as sharing an experience. An empathetic person would feel sad when others feel sad. They would feel pain when others feel pain, not just be sympathetic to pain.

4. Is emotional intelligence similar to cognitive reasoning?

Emotional intelligence has often been positioned as a type of intelligence right alongside cognitive ability. Cognitive ability (or the traditional type of intelligence that is measured with IQ tests) has been criticized because some feel that it does not encapsulate the full range of a human being's special abilities. Cognition is basically a formal way of saying "thinking," and the reader can think of it as including abilities like computation and spatial reasoning. Although there is not a consensus, some social scientists see emotional intelligence as being similar to cognition and just as important. Others argue that emotional intelligence is cognition that has been applied to emotions.

5. Can emotional intelligence be measured with tests the way that intelligence quotient (IQ) tests major cognitive ability?

There are several models of emotional intelligence and all have developed their own methods of measuring this capability. In part, this stems from an attempt to make emotional intelligence something measurable like IQ (a controversial subject itself). The development of these tests also reflects that emotional intelligence may have limited practical use in some circumstances if it cannot be measured. Some tests of emotional intelligence use self-report, which has been accused of being of limited utility as individuals can falsely report information in order to alter the results of the test.

6. Is there a benefit to organizations to invest in emotional intelligence training for their leadership pool?

Studies have suggested that 50% of managers are rated poorly by their employees. Further research in the area suggests this poor rating is at least in part related to the perception of lack of empathy from managers. Because of this, it has been suggested that emotional intelligence training can lead to improved leadership skills among management. Emotional intelligence training focuses on all the key areas of emotional intelligence: understanding one's own internal state, assessing the internal state of others accurately, feeling sympathy for others, and having empathy.

7. **Is there a reason why some people are better with empathy than others?**

There is a correlation between challenging life experiences and emotional intelligence, but some people seem to be blessed with great emotional intelligence from an early age, even with little life experience. Some may argue that certain people have "old souls" or that signs indicate that they have more experience than their years let one, but it is important to remember that emotional intelligence is an ability. Just as some people may have better cognitive ability naturally, some others may naturally be better at feeling empathy. This is not the end of the world. Anyone who recognizes that they need improvement in this area can foment change in their lives.

8. **What does it mean if some people lack emotional intelligence?**

Emotional intelligence is a capability that can be learned. This is part of the reason why studies have shown that organizations can benefit from investing in coaching and training for the leaders. Although some women and men may have better emotional intelligence skills in early life than others, we know that emotional intelligence skills and empathy can be learned because studies and anecdotal evidence suggest a correlation between this type of capability and life experience. Although there certainly are narcissists out there, we can rest at ease that human beings can change. Most people are able to approve their emotional intelligence skills with a little bit of pushing in the right direction.

Conclusion

The subject of emotion can be complex for people because some are not comfortable talking about emotion or do not know how to talk about emotion. In some cultures, it may be considered taboo to discuss matters of the heart while in others, individuals in positions of power are expected to show empathy to their subordinates as a matter of course. Cultural differences in matters of emotion are compounded by individual differences when it comes to the subject, with some feeling comfortable tapping into their emotional cookie jar and others not feeling as comfortable.

All of this makes the subject of emotional intelligence not an easy one to discuss. Emotional intelligence as a subject also suffers from a lack of consensus about how these skills should be defined and measured. Although most in the field agree that emotional intelligence should be considered a set of specific skills that are important in human interactions, there is not an agreement on what exactly those skills are. Fortunately, for the subject at hand, it can be agreed that empathy is an aspect of emotional intelligence that is important regardless of whichever model of emotional intelligence one chooses to support.

Empathy is the ability not only to have compassion and tolerance for others but to relate to and experience their subjective emotions. Sympathy and empathy are sometimes confused, but the ability to experiences another person's experiences is what distinguishes empathic feeling from sympathy. By having empathy rather than merely showing sympathy, individuals are able to connect with others in a deep way. This deep connection allows individuals to partake the many benefits of emotional intelligence, including the leadership advantages that have been shown time and time again in studies on the subject.

The purpose of this book has been to educate the reader on the subject of emotional intelligence in order to enable the reader to enjoy the benefits that being highly emotionally intelligent can confer.

Highly emotionally intelligent people are more successful in the workplace as managers and leaders. Highly intelligent children are rated higher by their teachers in performance and are liked and appreciated by their peers. Being emotionally intelligent has been shown to lead to more successful relationships, whether intimate, familiar, or otherwise. Because of these benefits, emotionally intelligent people live happy and fulfilled lives.

Recognizing one's emotions is the first step to becoming more emotionally intelligent, but it is important that this step is used in tandem with other steps to partake the full benefits of EI. Recognizing one's emotions alone is not enough to become highly emotionally intelligent, as this skill alone ignores the emotions of the other individual in an interaction, emotions that are just as important as one's own. People who recognize the emotions of others but do not then assess the other person's emotions and have no empathy for them run the risk of becoming narcissists, with all the life problems and societal dysfunction that comes along with that.

Much has been said about the role of emotional intelligence in daily life and whether we should treat it the same as we treat other forms of intelligence. Although there is a dispute about whether emotional intelligence should actually be considered intelligence, it has been shown convincingly that this skillset is a part of being human and interacting successfully with other humans. A point that has been stressed in this book is that problems people of today have in empathic awareness may be the cause of the sense of disconnectedness that people feel, as well as an overall perception that humans as a group may be moving in a "wrong" direction.

Interconnectedness is an essential part of being a human being and a member of the animal kingdom. Because we are humans, we are able to form bonds with others that come from perceptions of energy, whether that energy comes from emotions expressed or non-verbal communication. By being perceptive of the energies of others as well as our own, and by truly caring about the state that another person is in regardless of our personal stake in the matter, we are able to enjoy the benefits that come from the human patrimony: drawing from those intrinsic talents that we inherited from our ancestors and which we may never quite understand.

Copyright @2019 By Jeremiah Bonn

All Rights Reserved.

Made in United States
Orlando, FL
29 June 2023